On the Social and Emotional Lives of Gifted Children

Fourth Edition

On the Social and Emotional Lives of Gifted Children

Understanding and Guiding Their Development

Tracy L. Cross, Ph.D.

PRUFROCK PRESS INC.
WACO, TEXAS

Library of Congress Cataloging-in-Publication Data

Cross, Tracy L.
On the social and emotional lives of gifted children : understanding and guiding their development / Tracy L. Cross. -- 4th ed.
   p. cm.
Includes bibliographical references.
ISBN 978-1-59363-498-8 (pbk.)
1. Gifted children--Psychology. 2. Gifted children--Education. I. Title.
BF723.G5C76 2011
305.9'089--dc22

                          2010040312

Edited by Lacy Compton
Cover Design by Marjorie Parker
Production Design by Raquel Trevino

ISBN-13: 978-1-59363-498-8

Prufrock Press Inc.
P.O. Box 8813
Waco, TX 76714-8813
Phone: (800) 998-2208
Fax: (800) 240-0333
http://www.prufrock.com

TABLE OF CONTENTS

FOREWORD

The new edition of this book augurs well for expanding the audience who may be interested in the issues of social and emotional development of the gifted. It has added authors with different perspectives and topics that were not dealt with in the previous editions. Essays on topics like motivation, summer programs, acceleration, and talent development by noted scholars in the field provide capsulized views on issues relevant to the social and emotional development of gifted children. Another expansion is through the inclusion of columns that Dr. Cross has contributed to *Gifted Child Today* over the past several years on topics of interest to him in thinking about the issues of development of the gifted in affective ways. As a result, this book is more broadbased in its perspective and thus more interesting to read and consider.

Although the basic chapters contain anticipated information about the nature of the population, the key characteristics to be considered in social and emotional development, and the approaches that may be used to alleviate problems and guide development in healthy channels, they also suggest important new avenues for consideration. The suicide chapter suggests that, by inference, the population of gifted learners (along with other teenagers) who commit suicide has increased, and provides sound advice on how to cope with teens who exhibit warning signs. There is also a chapter on cutting, a self-mutilation technique common among teens including the gifted, and how to deal with that issue.

One especially good feature of the book is the careful way Cross ties the issues of the gifted to more normal development patterns, using Erikson's theory of adult development as a touchstone. He also tackles the various ways that technology impacts gifted learners, including their social and emotional lives, suggesting that communication in our current and future world has already been changed in fundamental ways by computers, and that the gifted are at the forefront of those changes.

The idea set forth in the last section of the book that the new metaphor for gifted youth is "life as entertainment" is an interesting thesis, and one that questions high-level accomplishment as the singular focus for the development of the gifted. In alignment with Carol Dweck's work on learning goals versus performance goals, Cross views the mindset of pursuing goals as superior to short-term performance, and striving for balance as the *summum bonum* of the life of a gifted child.

Gifted children are complex beings whose lives cannot be modulated by adults, as well-intentioned as the effort may be. They live intensely and transition rapidly from one situation to another. They set goals that may not be realizable, given the vagaries of modern-day life and their own mindsets. This book provides a fulcrum for the many adults who may wish to help them in their pursuit of excellence and life satisfaction, the twin pillars of desirable outcomes from gifted lives well-lived. While not providing answers to all of the questions we may have about social and emotional development of the gifted, the fourth edition of *On the Social and Emotional Lives of Gifted Children* does provide a focus on the right questions and issues. It should be read and reflected on for some time to come.

—Joyce VanTassel-Baska, Ed. D.,
Smith Professor Emerita,
College of William and Mary

PREFACE

I have always been a psychologist, an aspiring philosopher, and a closet poet. As a young child, I often pondered the nature of people—why some had to starve while others wasted resources, why some made friends so easily and others seemed to be left out, how it was possible that some incredibly nice, warm, and caring people could also be racists. Psyche had me from an early age. These same issues, in one form or another, still dominate my thinking today.

My best friend from age 3, Rick Allen, had an older brother named Ron, whom I could tell did not quite fit in with others. Although my friends occasionally made fun of him for being "different," the adults seemed to be both intrigued and entertained by him. I often watched him out of the corner of my eye, fascinated by this extraordinary young mind. He truly aspired to be President of the United States, but first he needed to go to Yale. Tall order for a 6-year-old! While my friends and I practiced football, Ron was creating plans for his ascent to the presidency. Ron did graduate from Yale University Law School, and he did become president, not of the United States, but rather of the International Young Trial Lawyers Association. Ron died in an unfortunate swimming accident at age 44. He lived a productive and meaningful life working on behalf of others. This book is in memory of Ron and the Allen family, one of the earliest and most important influences in my choosing this career path.

Other key events drew me into the field of gifted studies. As a teenager, I came to realize how bright my mother was. I also came to understand how the circumstances in her life—having grown up on a farm and graduating from a small rural high school as valedictorian at age 15—led her down a path of unrealized potential. An early marriage, four children in 6 years, and the typical sacrifices made by her generation of adults destined her to live her short 48 years as an unsung hero. The times and circumstances in which my mother grew up clearly limited her opportunities in life. This book is also dedicated to her memory. I am happy to report that, through funding from the Jacob K. Javits Grant and Advanced Placement Incentive programs, the

Indiana Academy for Science, Mathematics, and Humanities brought academic opportunities to high-ability students from modest backgrounds living in small rural communities. Students from 14 schools throughout Indiana benefitted from Project Aspire, and the trials of my mother's short life.

As a teenager, I had the fortune of working at my family's art gallery. I studied the artists who spent untold hours at the gallery interacting with Knoxville's "old money" and "nouveau riche." I learned from this experience that some extraordinarily talented people struggle to live by certain societal rules. I watched as several of these artists/professors at the local university self-destructed. I learned that society's expectations can be brutal reminders of the consequences of being gifted, but nonconforming.

My wife and I met while in high school. I became close to her gifted siblings—five children identified as academically gifted in one family. I studied them as I became a young man. Their vast differences were an early lesson for me about the diversity of people with gifts and talents.

In graduate school, I met Laurence J. Coleman (Larry). We worked together evaluating the Tennessee Governor's School Program and studied students' experiences of being gifted. Over the past 27 years, Larry and I have focused on the lives of gifted students in various types of settings and locations. We have produced numerous articles, chapters, and one textbook entitled *Being Gifted in School: An Introduction to Development, Guidance, and Teaching*. Larry's guidance and inspiration have been invaluable to me in my professional development.

While on faculty at the University of Wyoming, I made a lifelong friend in Roger Stewart. For 4 years, he and I burnt the midnight oil together working on numerous studies. Roger is a brilliant mind who does more to help other people than anyone I have met. He is a scholar and a gentleman. His influence on me is great.

This book was inspired by all of these important people who taught me many life lessons. The actual idea for creating this book, however, came from Sally Reis, who encouraged me to compile the columns I had written for *Gifted Child Today* (*GCT*) into a book. I am thankful to Sally for her kind words that led me to pursue this endeavor.

The text for this book was written over several years. The material, with one exception, is made up of the regular columns I wrote for *GCT*. The exception is an invited piece for *GCT* wherein a number of professionals in the field were asked to contribute our top 10 list of important events influencing the field of gifted education over the past century. New for this edition are essays written by some of my teachers. These professionals have made an important mark on my thinking so I wanted to highlight them in the book. They are seven very important professionals to the field of gifted studies: Laurence Coleman, Sal Mendaglio, Maureen Neihart, Nancy Robinson, Rena Subotnik, Paula Olszewski-Kubilius, and Mary Ann Swiatek. Their essays can be found throughout the book, delineated by the notation of "Special Commentary."

In total, there are 40 chapters on the social and emotional development of gifted students and the description of important events that have occurred over the past 100 years. They have been organized into four themes: "About Gifted Children: Who They Are and Why," "Guiding Gifted Children," "Gifted Children Today," and "Where We Have Been and Where We Are Going." Each includes key concepts at the beginning and discussion questions at the end.

The book concludes with a list of references and a Resources section that includes a comprehensive list of contact information for organizations, institutions, and other resources that will aid parents, counselors, and teachers across North America. I hope this book provides ideas that are helpful in understanding the social and emotional development of gifted students and how teachers, counselors, and parents can work together to guide their development.

Several people worked very hard to complete this edition of the book. I would like to thank Jennifer Cross and Steve Coxon for helping me during the project by editing, proofreading, and providing advice throughout the process. Jennifer also helped me during the original writing phase of the columns that appeared in *GCT*. Steve collaborated with me in the revision of the Continuum of Psychological Services. I also want to thank Joel McIntosh of Prufrock Press for supporting many of my efforts over the past 18 years. Steve Coxon, Xiaopeng Gong, and Judy Margison were instrumental in gathering the materials for the Resources section and providing assistance and wisdom throughout the revision process. A final note of thanks goes to my children, Ian, Keenan, Colin, and Eva, for reminding me on a daily basis of the importance of advocating for gifted students and the joy of being a parent.

INTRODUCTION

A Continuum of Psychological Services

- Continuum of Psychological Services
- Personal and professional biases

The social and emotional development of gifted students involves many issues and considerations. Those who have written on the subject during the past 25 years or so have tended to support the following claims:

- ◈ gifted students have social and emotional needs,
- ◈ gifted students' needs are often unique to them,
- ◈ there are specific characteristics of gifted students, and
- ◈ those characteristics create or reflect needs.

A much smaller group of authors has claimed that gifted students tend to experience life in ways similar to their nongifted peers. They also claim gifted students' social and emotional needs are often determined by the qualities of the environment in which they find themselves, and there are few, if any, characteristics that are identical in all gifted students. However, many authors agree that gifted children are, in fact, children first; that their early life experiences are important as they develop; and that parents have important roles to play in the social and emotional development of gifted students. Over the past 15 years, authors have encouraged the field of gifted education to focus more attention on the nonuniversal developmental patterns of students with gifts or talents and the different contexts in which gifted students exist (e.g., Coleman & Cross, 2001).

Growing interest has been seen in gifted students who manifest extraordinarily high IQ scores. These students have been called "profoundly," "severely," and "exceptionally" gifted. Although some data exists on those students (much of which is anecdotal from clinicians who provide therapeutic services to one or more of them), it is limited, and the nature and needs of this group of gifted students have not been fully documented.

To help provide a framework for understanding the ideas in this book, I have created a Continuum of Psychological Services (see Figure 1) that illustrates the wide range of needs gifted students have and the potential role that differing groups of adults undertake to help these students. The Continuum of Psychological Services (Cross, 2001) also makes evident that parents, teachers, and counselors need to work together to cover most of the services gifted students will need and that no one person can assume all of the roles described below. Newly revised and updated for this edition of the book, the continuum now better reflects both the interconnectedness of the individuals who guide gifted children and the complexity of their interactions.

In this continuum, advising is the broadest need area. This includes general life advice, such as how to choose a tie, and more specific information, such as what courses to consider taking. Because of the broad range of activities and the level of expertise needed to carry them out, many individuals will be capable of providing this service to gifted children. Parents tend to play a big role in these activities.

The guidance position is slightly more focused than advising, in that it usually deals mostly with academic or school-related matters. These can vary significantly from choosing course selections to building relationships. Although parents can provide this form of guidance to some extent, teachers are often key in providing such guidance to students on a daily basis. Guidance counselors provide this service to a few students and generally will do so with a higher level of professional preparation.

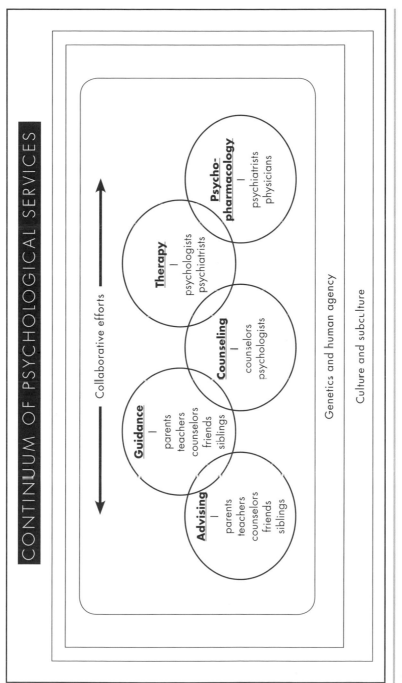

Figure 1. Continuum of Psychological Services

The counseling position requires more specific training in counseling theories and techniques than the advising and guidance positions. This category also overlaps with both the advising and therapy positions. It is different than the others because it naturally tends to revolve around school-based matters, and there is always a large built-in clientele for a school counselor or social worker.

The fourth position, therapy, is broader than counseling in the sense that it can pertain to almost any problem. It is different than counseling in that therapy can take years to complete, is typically done outside schools, and often involves seeing a therapist in a private setting. Therapy often deals with much more serious or dangerous problems than school counseling. I have placed the counseling and therapy headings in these two places on the continuum because, in many situations, counseling is primarily educative and therapy ameliorative, or working toward improvement. In essence, then, the continuum moves from general advice to trying to remedy behavioral problems via medication.

The final position on this continuum is psychopharmacology. This term reflects the current pattern in our culture of parents seeking medical treatments for behavioral problems. This pattern often yields some form of drug therapy, along with counseling-based treatments. Psychiatrists and family physicians typically deliver this type of service. However, referrals from parents, school psychologists, counselors, and social workers can also lead to students being treated with medications.

Although I recognize that my continuum of psychological services is rather elementary, the value of the continuum is that it illustrates the need for the collaboration of several groups of people. For example, if a parent has a concern about a child, it's possible that the child's teacher and others have some important information to share with parents. Without efforts of collaboration, parents and teachers can only hold one perspective of the child. Collaboration guarantees that multiple perspectives of the child, in differing settings, can be included in a discussion about that child's needs.

The next four sections of the book are a reflection of my thoughts on the lives of gifted students. I have tried to make it clear when I am reporting on research, or when I am offering my own opinion. These writings reflect my personal and professional predispositions. There is an eclectic nature I bring to the study of this phenomenon. To that end, I use psychological, educational, sociological, and anthropological data. I also draw on more than 30 years of serving gifted students in a variety of roles, including researcher, teacher, counselor, psychologist, administrator, and parent.

The last section of the book (Resources) has been updated for this edition. It provides information to parents, teachers, and counselors that enables them to get their questions answered locally. The resources provided represent the kinds of information that address the several thousand questions I have been asked over the past three decades. The information is also provided in an attempt to encourage the creation of networks of those interested in gifted children within states and across North America.

The following are a few assumptions and biases that I hold. They are offered to set the stage for the remainder of the book.

One bias I have is that all people live in differing subcultures that are very much impacted by the time in history in which they happen to grow up. Consequently, the study of gifted students must necessarily take these factors into consideration.

A second belief I have is that people are influenced by their own sense of human agency. And, although genetic predispositions clearly exist and are important, I believe that the developing person is able to change over time in ways that reflect an interaction with his or her environment. Consequently, the context in which gifted people live impacts their psychological development.

Another bias that influences my thinking is that I believe theories are just that—theories—educated social constructions subject to evolution over time with additional information and in differing contexts. I believe that giftedness must be considered in light of societal values and with an awareness of dominant subgroups. In an effort to transcend these biases, I try to seek many forms of data. I see skepticism as an important part of the interpretation of any theory or "statement of fact." I encourage all readers to develop a healthy sense of skepticism—not cynicism, but an ability to question what others may accept as fact.

This book represents my perspective on the social and emotional development of gifted children, colored by my training, experience, and beliefs.

FOR DISCUSSION

- What is the value of the Continuum of Psychological Services?

- Academic and school-related matters are mentioned as topics that would be addressed by individuals in a guidance position. Name issues/matters related to gifted students that might be addressed in other positions on the Continuum of Psychological Services.

- Reflect on and discuss the predispositions you bring to the topic of gifted children.

SECTION 1

About Gifted Children: Who They Are and Why

This section contains 9 chapters, all of which focus on a description of the gifted child. In my first column for *Gifted Child Today*, "Examining Beliefs About the Gifted," I felt it was important to present some information about how I have come to believe what I have about gifted children. The primary thrust of this chapter is that I do believe that there is such an entity as a gifted child and that we should be cautious not to impose one dominant perspective on our efforts to identify the social and emotional needs of this widely diverse group.

In the second chapter, "Determining the Needs of Gifted Children," I discuss the difficulty in determining the social and emotional needs or "issues" unique to gifted children. This is not an easy task. So much of what we believe on the matter has been determined before the completion of substantial research. In the next chapter, "Competing With Myths About the Social and Emotional Development of Gifted Students," I examine several of the myths about giftedness commonly held by parents, teachers, and administrators, as well as by gifted students. Challenging these myths is the first step in lessening the potentially negative effects on gifted students' social and emotional development.

A new chapter, "Social and Emotional Development of Gifted Children: Straight Talk," discusses eight issues that reflect current thinking on the social and emotional lives of gifted children that can be helpful to parents, teachers, and counselors who are in important positions to help these students develop.

Examining psychological theory also facilitates understanding a gifted child's development. Thus, in the fifth chapter, "Gifted Children and Erikson's Theory of Psychosocial Development," I overview Erik Erikson's eight stages of psychosocial development and relate them to the development of gifted children. I emphasize the need for adults to interpret a gifted child's behaviors in light of both Erikson's theory and a gifted child's idiosyncratic development and personal characteristics.

For years while interacting with gifted children, their parents, and their teachers, ideas about who gifted children are and what makes them different from others troubled me. I was finally able to draw many of these ideas together in a column that has become the sixth chapter, titled "A Consideration of Axiomatic Statements." These statements offer, in a nutshell, many of the principles underlying my beliefs about guiding gifted children. The notion that gifted children are children and people just like everyone else is an important one to remember for those who work with them. The exceptionality we see is not the *only* aspect of a child's development and may not even be the most significant one. These axiomatic statements provide a strong foundation for an understanding of the mixed messages gifted students receive on a daily basis.

The next chapter, "How Gifted Students Cope With Mixed Messages," takes a look at some of the research Larry Coleman and I have done into how gifted students deal with the expectations society places on them.

My research into the suicides of three students associated with a residential high school for gifted students led me to publish two columns on this very important and serious topic. The first of these, the chapter titled "Examining Claims About Gifted Children and Suicide," is placed in this section because of its emphasis on gifted adolescents who have committed suicide and how difficult it is to know more about these troubled children. It also attempts to provide guidance to adults about what can and should be done to prevent suicidal behavior in gifted students.

The final chapter, "On Chance and Being Gifted," examines the role of psychobiological, cultural, sociohistorical, and family influences on the lives of gifted children. This chapter may be especially meaningful to the parents of students with gifts and talents.

In addition, this section closes with the first three of many special commentaries scattered throughout this book: one by Laurence J. Coleman entitled "Being Gifted Is Abnormal?"; a second commentary essay by Sal Mendaglio, "Emotions and Giftedness"; and a third by Rena Subotnik, "Negotiating the Vicissitudes of Chance Factors." The chapters and special commentaries in this section will set the stage for an understanding of who gifted students are, and I hope they will give you pause as you examine your beliefs.

CHAPTER 1

Examining Beliefs About the Gifted

- Examining beliefs about the gifted
- The influence of the environment on the needs of gifted individuals

When I first began writing a regular column for *Gifted Child Today*, addressing issues pertaining to the social and emotional needs of gifted students, I felt it was appropriate to introduce myself in an effort to provide readers enough information to make an informed decision about whether or not to read the column. This is also important information for readers of this book.

I hold a doctoral degree in educational psychology from the University of Tennessee–Knoxville. My original training was very quantitative, or objective, in nature. Later, however, I took additional coursework and also apprenticed for 3 years under a phenomenologist. I have been a college professor at a land grant university, three state universities, and a small liberal arts college and have studied gifted students throughout the nation. For approximately a decade, I served as the executive director for a state-funded residential school for academically gifted adolescents. Since then, I continued to supervise the gifted residential school and a K–12 laboratory school for 4 years, and worked as Associate Dean for Graduate Studies, Research and Assessment, and as the George and Frances Ball Distinguished Professor of Psychology and Gifted Studies, all at Ball State University. Most recently, I serve The College of William and Mary as the Jody and Layton Smith Professor of Psychology and Gifted Education and as the Executive Director of the Center for Gifted Education. Even though I realize that this information is far more interesting to me than it is to you, I am quite sure that each of these facts has influenced my views of the world. So, *caveat emptor!*

In the *GCT* columns and in this book, I tried to provide information and ideas that would pique the interest of some, prompt hallway conversations among some, and, perhaps, raise the dander of others. To that end, my approach varies from offering basic factual information, to arguing others' points, to reporting on studies I have conducted. I try to present at least two major lines of thought on important topics and often try to situate the focus of each chapter within research, while at the same time elucidating concerns about how we have come to hold certain beliefs. To reach these goals, I tried to write the columns adapted into this book in a style that would be accessible to as large an audience as possible.

Clarifying Beliefs About the Gifted

The topic of discussion, the social and emotional needs of gifted students, presupposes some important beliefs, including:

- ❖ gifted people do exist;
- ❖ they are identifiable;
- ❖ we have established a process to identify them, and consequently, we have identified them (at least enough of them to educate our biases);
- ❖ those we have identified represent the real thing; and
- ❖ once we have identified them, we can make reasonable decisions about what their social and emotional needs are.

Is there evidence that gifted people do exist? At this point, I feel quite comfortable in claiming that most educators would acknowledge that some people manifest extraordinary abilities. We have heard of or personally know people who seem to read better, run faster, jump higher, do high-level mathematics before they can talk, paint remarkable works of art, or play the piano masterfully at an early age. In short, human variation stares us in the face every day of our lives. Hence, gifted people do seem to exist.

There are at least two approaches we use to come to grips with the manifest differences across people. The first is to conclude that people who do not demonstrate the exceptional qualities previously listed are less than adequate, while the second approach is to label the aforementioned people as exceptional and call them *gifted*. I like the second option better myself. As reasonable as this logic may seem on the surface, the decision to establish nongifted folks as normal has some important intellectual baggage. For example, when I think of the term *needs* (as in social and emotional needs of the gifted), I reflect upon my upbringing when my parents would attempt to teach me a lesson. The lesson usually began with a statement like "Tracy, you need to . . . " I remember thinking, "According to you, I may need to, but to me I am OK with the way I am currently doing it."

In short, by establishing the gifted as different, we become normal, thus elevating ourselves into the position of deciding what gifted people need.

The term *needs* is considered by some as a direct reflection of the values of a dominant group in society. Moreover, much of the research conducted on this topic has been done over the past 60 years. During this time, many groups of people (e.g., Native Americans, African Americans, Hispanic Americans) have been conspicuously missing from the ranks of those identified as gifted. Therefore, we should be aware of the historical context and the absence of voice reflected in many of the studies seeking to shed light on the needs of gifted children.

Defining Terms

One of the difficult aspects of being considerate when trying to understand the social and emotional needs of gifted students is that these needs may not be static. That is to say, the environment in which students live and learn may greatly impact these needs.

In short, at this point in history we can say that serious consideration must be given to the terminology used to describe gifted students and its relationship to cultural power, the voices that are missing from the dialogue, and the relative influence or determination of environmental factors on the nature of the needs of the gifted. Food for thought.

So, as we continue this dialogue, I assert that we should constantly remind ourselves to question from whose perspective we are establishing and defining the social and emotional needs of gifted students.

FOR DISCUSSION

- Reflect on and discuss how the inclusion of North American minority groups (e.g., Native Americans, African Americans, Hispanic Americans) in gifted education research may change prevailing beliefs.

- Discuss how the environment may impact the needs of a gifted individual.

Determining the Needs of Gifted Children

- Buescher's developmental framework
- Social and emotional needs/issues of gifted versus nongifted children
- Cultural influences on gifted children

This chapter will pick up where the first one left off by posing two questions frequently asked about gifted students: Do gifted students really have social and emotional needs and, if they have these needs, are they the same as those of their nongifted peers?

For years, researchers, clinicians, and educators have tried to untangle the complicated relationships among the general ability, family dynamics, specific culture, and school experiences of children in order to build models of the social and emotional development of gifted children. From the various studies conducted and the research techniques employed in these studies, I feel it has been established that children do develop emotionally and socially and, consequently, do have needs or (perhaps more appropriately stated) issues in these areas. An important contribution to the research base is by Thomas Buescher (1985)—an article entitled "A Framework for Understanding the Social and Emotional Development of Gifted and Talented Students." In this article, he outlined a developmental framework to be used for identifying social and emotional concerns of gifted students. The framework includes six "Dynamic Issues of Giftedness During Adolescence":

◈ Ownership: Who says I am gifted anyhow?

❖ Dissonance: Recurrent tension between my performance and my own expectations.

❖ Risk-taking: Should I be taking new risks or seeking secure situations?

❖ Others' expectations: Being pushed by others' expectations, being pulled by my own needs.

❖ Impatience: I have to know the answer right now!

❖ Identity: What counts is who I am. (p. 14)

This framework allows us to identify possible needs of gifted children based upon the qualities and issues relevant to the individual child, rather than trying to create an all-encompassing list of needs for all gifted children. This is an important point and will be discussed as part of the response to the second question.

Now, on to the question about whether the social and emotional needs of gifted children are different from those of their nongifted peers. There are two lines of thought on this question. The traditional consideration is that differences need to be ferreted out if they exist, which suggests the importance of distinctions being made between gifted and nongifted children. The alternative consideration is that it really matters not whether the differences exist as long as the phenomenon of what gifted children's social and emotional needs are has been captured and depicted. In short, this alternative focuses on what is needed for gifted children without regard for their nongifted peers. One of the reasons this debate is important is that the two research positions often lead to differing research approaches. In turn, the approaches define what can be known about the social and emotional needs of gifted children. And, like viewing the world through an eye patch on either the right or left eye, one's perception of reality is always attenuated by the view.

I believe that there is not sufficient evidence to unequivocally claim that gifted children have social and emotional needs that are qualitatively different from, or mutually exclusive of, those of their nongifted peers. Having said this, I will discuss two issues that I think are critical to my position. The first was noted previously: The search for a list of needs that cut across all gifted children is misguided. The second is that the differences in needs are likely a function of the relationship of the individual child's talents and his or her social interactions within the prominent communities of his or her world (e.g., family and school).

In the politics of research exploration, there is a desire to build a model or list of needs encompassing all children. This goal fuels and is fueled by the common wisdom, myths, and speculation about what gifted children's needs might be. In my opinion, not enough consideration has been given to other qualities and experiences the gifted child has that would influence his or her needs. For example, lists abound of the nature and needs and the characteristics of gifted children. These lists include claims that are always wide-ranging and often inconsistent. And, at the same time, we have all known students who fit some or much of the information not on the list. To rectify this situation, I recommend we redefine the concern of *need* by using the term Buescher and others have used, *issue*. The question would then change to "What are the social and emotional issues of gifted children?"

As the research base on the social and emotional development of gifted children grows, along with the evolving research approaches being taken, a clear message is emerging. That is, the culture in which a child is immersed has an important influence on the experience of being gifted. The cultural values interact with the social goals of the student and the issues associated with growing up in America. In short, although the characteristics of the gifted child, along with certain environmental factors, might create conditions where needs should exist, unless the individual child perceives or experiences the needs, they do not exist—no matter what a list might include or an expert might say.

So, what can we say? Where can we turn for reasonable information? I suggest that, if you are interested in reviewing some of the salient research on the topic that reflects these two lines of thought, you should consider the following authors. Dr. Linda K. Silverman is a leader in the field who has written a textbook on counseling the gifted, in which she discussed her beliefs about what the social and emotional needs are and how to address them from a clinician's perspective. Laurence J. Coleman represents an alternative line of thinking that can be reviewed in his 1985 textbook, *Schooling the Gifted*, and in miscellaneous articles (e.g., "Is Being Gifted a Social Handicap?" [1988], which I coauthored).

Coleman has emphasized the influence the relationship between the environment of a school and the gifted child's desire to feel accepted in the environment has on his or her social and emotional needs. Both Silverman and Coleman are fine researchers who provide worthwhile perspectives on the social and emotional needs of gifted children.

FOR DISCUSSION

- How would you respond to an individual who asserts that research into the social and emotional needs of gifted children should focus on determining how their needs differ from those of nongifted children?

- Discuss the idea that immersion in a particular culture has an impact or influence on the experience of being gifted.

CHAPTER 3

Competing With Myths About the Social and Emotional Development of Gifted Students

- Myths about giftedness have negative effects on the social and emotional development of gifted students.
- Myth 1: Gifted students should be with students their own age.
- Myth 2: Gifted students should be in same-age heterogeneous classes.
- Myth 3: Gifted students should be perfectly well-rounded.
- Myth 4: Being gifted is something you are just born with.
- Myth 5: Everyone is an expert in giftedness.
- Myth 6: Adults know what gifted students experience.
- Myth 7: Being too smart in school is a problem, especially for girls.
- Myth 8: All kids are gifted/no kids are gifted.

As a person who has dedicated himself to the study of the psychological and experiential lives of gifted students, I have encountered several widely held myths and associated practices that have negative effects on the social and emotional development of gifted students. These myths are common among parents, teachers, administrators, and gifted students. As a wise person (Lao Tsu) once said, "Nothing is more difficult than competing with a myth." Doing so, however, can create tremendous opportunities for people. Recall that it was not that long ago that myth prevented women from competing in long-distance foot races.

The following list includes some of the most common and insidious examples of myths pertaining to the social development of gifted students. I hope that by discussing these examples, gifted students will be better served and barriers to their well-being will be broken.

Myth 1: Gifted Students Should Be With Students Their Own Age

The worry expressed here is that something inappropriate will occur if different age groups spend time together. Parents, teachers, and administrators worry that such groups of multiage children will struggle with exploitation, intimidation, inappropriate modeling, and sexuality. This prevailing myth supports some advocates' preferences for educational models that emphasize enrichment rather than acceleration. Their logic is as follows: "We should keep the students together even if they have already mastered the material." Some believers of this myth will claim that research supports this point, but in fact they are mistaken. Writers have published this sentiment, but research does not support this idea. In fact, in my research with Larry Coleman, it is clear that gifted students need opportunities to be with their intellectual peers, no matter their age difference (Coleman & Cross, 2001). Although there are plenty of appropriate reasons to provide enriching educational experiences, these decisions should not be made out of fear, worry, or myth; they should be based on the needs of the students.

Myth 2: Gifted Students Are Better Off if They Spend Their Entire School Day Amidst Same-Age, Heterogeneous Classmates

The claim is that if we allow gifted students to be clustered together through one of any means available, they will be unable to get along with others later in life, and this experience will cause emotional distress. Middle school principals and some middle school teachers regularly express these feelings. This concern includes many adults' beliefs that gifted students, to be happy, must become socially astute. Becoming socially astute requires that gifted students spend as much time as possible in heterogeneous, or mixed-ability, classroom environments. Once again, the claimed research that supports this myth is virtually nonexistent. Imagine all of the opportunities students have to interact with other people outside of school. Church, sports, clubs, meals, and camps are just a few examples. Sacrificing learning and creating frustration based on this myth is unethical, in my opinion. This problem increases as students develop and their knowledge base increases within a specific discipline.

Myth 3: Being Perfectly Well-Rounded Should Be the Primary Goal for Gifted Student Development

Please note the carefully chosen phrase "perfectly well-rounded," as opposed to "somewhat well-rounded." Many parents, teachers, and administrators believe that it is their role to ensure that gifted students are perfectly well-rounded. To that end, they will encourage, prod, goad, push, threaten, and yell at gifted students to get them to spend less time engaged in their passion areas and more time engaged in something the adult wishes them to do. A very common example is that of an introverted gifted student who has great facility with computers. Adults will drag the child away from her passion to get her to participate in something she may loathe. Although adults in each of these roles should be concerned with the well-being of gifted students, requiring them to engage in activities for which the gifted student has no interest (e.g., going outside and playing or spending time with other children she does not choose to play with during the school day) as a means to make them happy later in life is misguided. Much of the research on successful gifted adults has revealed that they spent considerable amounts of time, often alone, working in their areas of passion as children. A more reasonable approach is to encourage and nurture other interests in the child, rather than sending them the message that they are unacceptable as they are. For example, sending gifted children to a residential summer program can do wonders to broaden their interests within a community where they feel emotionally safe and accepted for who they are. Parents should be clear when they ask their gifted child to try to make new friends whether or not he or she *needs* new friends.

Myth 4: Being Gifted Is Something With Which You Are Just Born

A corollary to this is the idea that things come easily when you are gifted, or that being gifted means never having to study or try hard in school. This naïve notion of giftedness, while intuitively proper, can be debilitating to gifted students' development. Many teachers, parents, administrators, and gifted students hold this belief. It is not backed, however, by research on talent development or development in general. Moving from an *entity* notion of giftedness to an *incremental* notion, wherein talent is developed with hard work and some failure, is a much healthier and more nurturing experience of being a gifted student (Dweck, 1986). This change in understanding of giftedness is of particular importance before age 10 or so. That is because a school's curriculum tends to get more focused as it moves toward middle school. Many gifted students experience this change as personal failure, causing self-doubt and distress, because they have internalized intellectual struggle as failure. To change this belief merely requires teaching gifted students about the two definitions, exposing them to models who failed in the process of great accomplishment (e.g., Thomas Edison), and having them go through processes that include struggle as part of growth.

Myth 5: Virtually Everybody in the Field of Gifted Education Is an Expert on the Social and Emotional Development of Gifted Students

An extension of this is that every adult (parent, teacher, school administrator) is an expert on the social and emotional development of gifted students. The field of gifted studies is quite small, often yielding professionals in the field who are called on to be experts in numerous areas. This regularly plays out with a high percentage claiming expertise and being called on to provide wisdom on this topic. Another reason for this situation is the fact that we were all students once ourselves, and that fact supposedly makes us familiar with gifted students' lives. This is similar to my having played football as a youngster, and now claiming expertise equivalent to that of Peyton Manning. Many factors combine to create situations where competing advice—sometimes by people who mean well, but do not know the research on the social and emotional development of gifted students—is given. As the field of gifted studies grows and matures, I think that children would be better served by having the expertise of those who specialize in the study of their needs, rather than relying on a model that requires its experts to know a little about everything associated with the field.

Myth 6: Adults (Parents, Teachers, and Administrators) Know What Gifted Students Experience

In addition to the usual generational differences, in many ways, contemporary experiences are different from the experiences of previous generations. For example, many gifted students go to school fearful of schools as unsafe environments. Gifted students today are often surrounded by guns, and when they are not, often still perceive that they are. In short, the vague red menace of previous generations has been replaced by generalized anxiety and fear, fear that the media has exacerbated and kept alive in ways that are inescapable by today's youth. The hubris of adults who believe they know what gifted students experience on a daily basis is mind-boggling. Consider these two facts: The suicide rate of adolescents rose more than 240% between 1955 and 1990, and suicide is the second leading cause of death of this age group (Holinger, Offer, Barter, & Bell, 1994). Is it possible that our children live in a somewhat different context than current adults did at the same age? If parents can observe classrooms more often, and talk with their gifted children, asking for descriptions of their experiences, then a much richer understanding of what these students experience is possible.

Myth 7: Being Too Smart in School Is a Problem, Especially For Girls

This myth has many facets to it. It represents adults' worries about their own feelings of acceptance; concerns about fears associated with standing out; the typical anti-intellectual culture of schools; the reflection of society's undervaluation of high levels of achievement; and the often mentioned, intuitively based association of high levels of intellectual ability with low levels of morality. The obvious consequence of this myth is the nurturing of incredibly high percentages of our students who underachieve in school. A large proportion of American students with gifts and talents have developed social coping strategies that take up time and energy, limit their opportunities, cause them to make bad decisions, retard their learning, and threaten their lives. These behaviors and beliefs make perfect sense when one perceives the mixed messages about being gifted in their school's social milieu. We must provide support for these children as they navigate the anti-intellectual contexts in which they spend much of their time.

Myth 8: All Kids Are Gifted, and No Kids Are Gifted

This myth is most often expressed by administrators and occasionally by teachers. The reasons for these two beliefs are predictable given the developmental differences that manifest across grade levels. For example, while in the elementary grades, which are thought to have a more amorphous curriculum than the later grades, teachers typically perceive manifestations of potential for extraordinary work as indicators of giftedness. As the child moves toward high school, where the curriculum tends to be quite focused, with distinct disciplines being taught by teachers passionate about the subject areas they teach (we hope), giftedness is often determined as meaningful only as a manifestation of success within the specific courses. Middle school represents some of both of these operative definitions of giftedness.

Another important aspect of this belief is the primary motivator that led teachers and administrators to pursue their profession. For example, when you ask elementary teacher candidates what they want to do most, they will tell you that they want to teach young children. Secondary teachers tend to say that they want to teach math, English, and so forth. Middle school teachers often hold very strong views about the specific age group of students with whom they have chosen to work. These teachers and administrators often describe the primary school-based needs of middle school students in terms of social needs and their need to learn in a protective environment that emphasizes the students' developmental frailties. A rigorous educational curriculum is seldom the highest priority.

Another undercurrent to these positions is that being gifted is tied to the assumption that gifted children are better than other students. This is a very unfortunate connection, because it encourages adults to hold the position that either all kids are gifted, or no kids are gifted. James Gallagher, a wise man in the field of gifted education, once said, "When someone claims that all kids are gifted, merely ask them 'In what?'" Being gifted eventually has to be in something. Although all kids are great, terrific, valuable, and depending on your beliefs, perhaps even gifts from God, they are not all gifted in the way the term is used in the field. Giftedness is not an anointment of value. Someone who shows extraordinary ability for high levels of performance when young and who has been provided appropriate opportunities to demonstrate talent development that exceeds normal levels of performance is gifted.

I hope that providing a list of some of the pervasive and insidious myths that affect the lives of gifted students will inspire us to take action on behalf of these students. If we challenge these myths with examples of good research, provide appropriate counseling, and create learning environments where students with gifts and talents can thrive, then many of these myths can be eliminated.

FOR DISCUSSION

- A number of myths about gifted students and giftedness are discussed. Discuss instances when you (as a parent, teacher, or counselor) taught, guided, or counseled a gifted child based on information that you now know is a myth. How would you handle a similar situation now?

- Based on the myths discussed, how would you (as a teacher, parent, or counselor) change your practices?

CHAPTER 4

Social and Emotional Development of Gifted Children: Straight Talk

KEY CONCEPTS

- Are all students gifted?
- Are gifted students weak?
- How do we define giftedness?
- Is giftedness an entity or incremental development?
- How should we parent gifted students?
- What is the relationship of giftedness with diversity?
- Do gifted adolescents have a need for authenticity?
- The call to act on behalf of gifted students

In the past year, I have been asked during interviews on two different occasions what message I would like to convey directly to parents, teachers, and counselors of gifted children. Consequently, I have had a fair amount of time to think about this and have developed a list of eight topics I think are important enough to speak to quite directly.

1. The first topic that I would like to address is the question "Are all students gifted?" The answer to this question is no. As Jim Gallagher has said on many occasions, "Gifted in what?" To be gifted, one must ultimately be gifted in something. All children are wonderful. They are considered in many cultures as the most valuable beings in the world. Even so, they are not gifted by the profession's definitions. Giftedness is a sci-

entific construct that has a relatively circumscribed definition. Therefore, only a small portion of children would actually be identified as gifted.

2. Students with gifts and talents are as equally mentally and physically healthy (if not more so) as the general population of students. Studies in the United States going back 80 or more years, along with multiple more recent studies, have illustrated this fact again and again. Even in very specific areas such as suicidal behavior, recent research has shown that suicide ideation among the gifted is at the same level or less than that of the general population. And, while we do not know for sure in terms of prevalence rates of completed suicide, significant differences between the general population and students with gifts and talents have not been shown.

3. This third issue is difficult to describe as it deals with how we come to know about gifted children. Who are the gifted, and how do we come to find them? We tend to define giftedness as children who require a special education. We tend to identify them on the basis of their potential or abilities for outstanding performance in the future. Then, over time, we anoint them as gifted or talented on the basis of their achievement in a specific domain.

4. Although these three emphases of definition, identification, and recognition seem quite similar, in fact they are different. With young students who have verbal skills, we typically find them with some indication on a standardized test or a hint a teacher picks up on. This is really an effort to predict the future by determining that a child has a need warranting a special education. Then we bring to bear what we can in terms of teaching, curriculum, and other opportunities to develop these potentialities into talent areas such as mathematics, language arts, and the like. The primary problem is that we know there are influences on each of these three areas, including social class. So, economic status tends to end up being a very important variable that prevents us from identifying and providing the services these children need to be successful. This is very

important given the increasing diversity in our country. This is, in my opinion, the most important issue of our day—finding and servicing all of the children with gifts and talents.

5. Another very important issue is the fact that many of us have changed our views about what giftedness is, from that of an entity, meaning something that one is born with, to a phenomenon that is incremental in its development. Professionals including Carol Dweck have written about this way of thinking. The incremental model is much more representative of what actually takes place in a person's life from birth until death relative to developing specific skills. Across the lifespan, people receive instruction, struggle with some failure, and develop knowledge and skills. This is a much healthier notion to guide the efforts of a parent, teacher, or counselor in terms of the work we do on behalf of our children. We should not think of them as fully formed because someone has anointed them as gifted (entity model). Rather, we should think of gifted children as requiring a special education now and over time. With our expertise being brought to bear, gifted children will hopefully reach their full potential.

6. The fifth topic is parenting and the development of students with gifts and talents. The research base here over the years has been rather meager, but it is growing. We know from research on the development of children in general that there are predictable outcomes of parenting styles and approaches. As we continue to pursue the development of students with gifts and talents, we need to conduct considerable research in this area so we can better guide and prepare parents to work with children. Engaging children in dialogue that accentuates communication, while at the same time helping them individuate, can lead to high levels of agency and greater life successes. Until the research base in this area expands, however, we would be wise to draw on the best practices of parenting research in general. We also can draw from research investigating the lived experiences of gifted students and how they cope with their lives in school. These two databases will shed light on parenting issues.

With gifted studies research, we should carefully monitor the growing research bases on perfectionism and resiliency and gifted students. Insights about parenting students with gifts and talents, while in its early stages, are being revealed, holding great promise for guiding parenting practices in the future.

7. The next issue is diversity and giftedness. There is so much yet to know about diversity and gifted students that we are just scratching the service. All groups of people have samples within them who have outstanding potential to develop into great talents within and outside of the traditional cultures they represent. Moreover, as we become more diverse as a country, this fact has become increasingly obvious in some areas such as the visual arts, where there is a physical manifestation of emerging talent that most adults can recognize. It is easy to garner the resources to support these students while other talent domains, such as early mathematic potential or logic, take a while to reveal themselves in a manner that the general population can understand. So much work needs to be done in the area of diversity and giftedness to maximize the potential of all students.

8. An interesting corollary to the diversification of America intersecting with the technology evolution is playing out socially among our students. We have been living through fascinating changes in American culture over the past 20 years or so as an evolution of technologies in terms of laptop computers, desktop computers, and, more recently, gaming, has occurred to the extent in which people from all walks of life participate in these activities. One of the manifestations of this evolution has been the change of the language associated historically with gifted children, such as being called a *nerd*, *geek*, *brainiac*, or any number of other things. This evolution where gifted children often are top competitors in games, in fixing computers, or in setting up technologies has raised their status in the general population. Stores have Geek Squads, and adults will use the term *geek* or *nerd* as an adjective rather than a noun. I think it is showing that as our country becomes more diverse, being an academically or intellectually gifted person gets defined in the

broad context and over time is becoming less of a problem for gifted people as compared to what it was 50 or even 20 years ago.

9. True for the general population of adolescents, and especially true for some gifted adolescents, is the desire for authenticity among the adults they deal with. In my work at the Indiana Academy, I observed that many intellectually gifted adolescents desired their interactions to be absolutely authentic. When gifted children assess that an adult person is not being authentic—genuine—not only do they devalue that person, but it causes them conflict in trying to make sense out of the importance they ascribe to adults and the authentic behavior. For some of these gifted young people, they conclude that most people are inauthentic most of the time, that the only true feeling is that of pain, and that every other feeling state is more manufactured than authentic. There are all sorts of negative ramifications to the belief that this feeling, state of pain, is the only genuine one. One of the results is that students will find ways to feel pain so they can feel themselves to be authentic, so they have feelings they can identify, and so they can gain a sense of relief. We know from our research that cutting behavior among our youth, adolescents, and young adults has increased quite a bit in the last 20 years and, in my opinion, is quite likely associated in some cases with this desire for authenticity.

10. The last important issue is that it is incumbent upon us as adults to act proactively on behalf of students with gifts and talents. The important point here is that we should all feel morally obligated to act on behalf of students with gifts and talents because not to do so is, in fact, choosing not to act. Inaction has all sorts of consequences for gifted students in terms of their not being challenged in school, feeling frustrated, feeling unvalued, feeling like there is something wrong with them, and so forth. We cannot be guilty of turning a blind eye to the social and emotional issues and needs of students with gifts and talents.

If we do nothing, we become complicit in the decline of their psychological well-being.

One approach to engaging others is for us to use language that does not pit us against our colleagues. For example, when we talk about students with gifts and talents, we should frame our conversation within the goal set that our schools should aspire to all students maximizing their potential, including gifted children. This will allow a different kind of conversation to be held than often occurs. This goal for students runs counter to the minimum-competency testing common to the U.S. Changing the conversation from minimum competency to maximizing the potential of all students will dramatically affect the opportunities for all students, including those with gifts and talents.

The social and emotional development of students with gifts and talents lasts a lifetime. We have learned many important lessons about how to help them develop during their school-age years and with this newfound knowledge have a corresponding responsibility to act. The eight issues discussed in this column bring to light some of the current thinking that can be helpful to those of us (parents, teachers, counselors) who are in important positions to help them develop. Understanding what giftedness actually is and is not and how to identify it, moving from an entity model of giftedness to an incremental model, continuing to strive to be as effective a parent as one can be, and understanding the needs of authenticity enable adults to assist in the social and emotional development of students with gifts and talents.

FOR DISCUSSION

- Discuss differing models of the following: understanding the relationships between the definitions of giftedness that we employ; whom we identify and whom we do not identify as gifted; how what we believe about diversity is important to our gifted children's future.

- What are the ramifications of switching from an entity model to an incremental model?

- What are the ramifications of believing that all children are gifted? What does this mean for schools?

CHAPTER 5

Gifted Children and Erikson's Theory of Psychosocial Development

KEY CONCEPTS

- Erikson's theory of psychosocial development has eight developmental stages.
- Psychosocial development is facilitated by resolving crises.
- Erikson's view of the development of one's identity is important in the overall development of people.

In this chapter, I will provide an introduction to one of the most influential thinkers in the field of psychology, Erik Erikson. After I overview his theory of psychosocial development, I will tie it to the development of gifted children. Erikson was a young contemporary of Sigmund Freud, the father of psychoanalysis. Erikson discussed growing up in Europe with one biological parent being Jewish and the other Gentile. He described himself as being a tall, blonde-haired, blue-eyed person with a big nose. He said that people in the Jewish community called him "the goy" (non-Jew), while those in the Gentile community called him "the Jew" (Erikson, 1972).

As he grew, he came to feel that he had experienced a crisis of identity. After studying children, Erikson forwarded a theory of psychosocial development. His theory had as its core the notion of developmental stages through which a crisis must be resolved. His theory established

27

a framework for understanding the typical psychosocial developmental patterns of people. It broke with traditional thinking of psychologists of the period, which held that people's identity development ceased after adolescence. Erikson's theory claimed that people continue to develop across their lifespans. Another important feature of Erikson's theory was that it postulated that a person's id (the part of the mind containing basic needs and feelings) is free from internal conflict but susceptible in its development to psychosocial conflict, not internal psychosexual conflict as Freud had claimed. Erikson meant that conflict arises not from the internal forces of the person, but rather from the person's interaction with his or her environment. Indeed, culture is important to a person's development. This position was undoubtedly influenced by Erikson's interactions with Margaret Mead.

Erikson defined eight developmental stages during which a crisis must be resolved in order for a person to develop psychosocially without carrying forward issues tied to the previous crisis. During the infancy stage (the first year of life), he proposed that the primary crisis to be resolved is one of *trust versus mistrust*. Erikson labeled the task to be resolved during the second year of life (toddler stage) as *autonomy versus shame and doubt*; the preschooler stage (years 3–5), as *initiative versus guilt*; and the elementary school stage as *competence versus inferiority*. As a child moves into adolescence, he or she must refine his or her sense of *identity versus role confusion*; in young adulthood, his or her sense of *intimacy versus isolation*; in middle adulthood, the sense of *generativity versus despair*; and in older age, his or her sense of *integrity versus despair*. According to Erikson, as the individual negotiates a crisis at each stage of development, basic strengths or virtues emerge. The following are the eight basic virtues that Erikson believed emerged across psychosocial development: hope, will, purpose, competence, fidelity, love, care, and wisdom, respectively.

I have come to believe that Erikson's view of the development of one's identity is very important in the overall development of people. I also have come to believe that the previous and subsequent stages of development (stages 1–4 and 6–8) are influenced by this drive to establish an identity. Because we are discussing the lives of gifted students, I will focus on the stages (1–5) of typical school-age children.

As parents, teachers, and counselors, we are often the significant adult figures in the lives of gifted children. To guide their psychosocial development, we should pay great attention to the crises Erikson described as occurring during the first 18 years of life. For example, during the infancy stage, parents are the primary caregivers who see that the basic needs of the child are met. Food, shelter, and proactive efforts at comforting the infant lead it to hold a basic trust about the world. When children's needs are not met at this critical early stage, an imbalance of mistrust results and sets the stage for a child's basic mistrust of his or her environment and those in it.

As children continue to grow and become toddlers, they grapple with issues of autonomy. If encouraged to explore age-appropriate and accomplishable tasks, they will develop a heightened sense of autonomy. In Western society, a common term used to describe children of this age is "the terrible twos." Although it is quite clear that the increase in physical movement and experimentation is physiologically based, as parents of children in this age group, we often experience their behavior as "terrible." This experience on the part of the parents can lead them to discourage their children's explorations of their world. If discouraged, or if children explore their world with no regard for age-appropriate tasks, they will develop self-doubt and shame. Once again, imagine how people's lives differ if they operate from a strong sense of autonomy or from self-doubt and shame.

Between the ages of 3–5 (the preschooler stage), children attempt to find the balance between striking out on their own (initiative) and fearing to do so (guilt). As adults, it is important to encourage children's early efforts at self-initiating behavior. For example, if young children indicate a willingness to pursue activities, either independent of their parents or just beyond their previous successes, parents need to encourage the behavior. If children do not learn it is acceptable or advisable for them to initiate activities on their own, then they begin to feel guilty. It is sad to see a 5-year-old child who manifests a heightened sense of guilt.

Identification of giftedness is often linked to early evidence of ability. The potential success of any identification process to locate children of extraordinary ability is often subject to the extent to which children have developed a sense of autonomy and engage in self-initiating behaviors. According to Erikson, not successfully resolving the crises of the previous three states will have a negative impact on later life. In addition, the culmination of not resolving the crises will reduce the likelihood of children being identified as gifted.

During the elementary school stage of Erikson's theory, ages 6–12, the child's psychosocial crisis is that of competence versus inferiority. Clearly, teachers, counselors, and parents all have a stake in and the possibility of positively affecting the child's development during this stage. It is important that the group of adults works together to see that gifted students have ample opportunities to successfully complete meaningful work. This should not be limited to in-school activities. The meaningful nature of the work is crucial, but unfortunately often missing from what adults expect or tolerate in gifted children's lives. Adults should anticipate several successful efforts on the part of the child before the child's internal assessment of being competent will be affected. As the child successfully completes tasks, adults need to provide variation in both task and location of the activities.

According to Erikson, during adolescence, a primary aspect of developing one's identity deals with role confusion. Puberty disrupts the predictability and understandings an individual has developed as a child, and the search for identity is the paramount psychosocial experience for the adolescent. Often, cliques form and manifest exclusionary behavior. Everyone who passed through adolescence was affected to some extent by this search for identity. This "over identification" with a desired group is actually "a defense against a sense of identity confusion" (Erikson, 1972, p. 262). Adolescents search for who they are. Their determination is made by attempting to integrate what they believed themselves to be as children, their newly discovered libidos, and their vision of their future selves. Erikson (1972) stated that the adolescent mind is essentially a mind of the moratorium—a psychosocial stage between childhood and adulthood (i.e., the morality learned by the child and the ethics to be developed by the adult). It is an ideological mind. Indeed, it is the ideological outlook of a society that speaks most clearly to the adolescent who is eager to be affirmed by his peers and is ready to be confirmed by rituals, creeds, and programs that at the same time define what is evil, uncanny, and inimical (Erikson, pp. 262–263).

Gifted adolescents develop a sense of self through various interactions with groups of people. Erikson called this "trying on different hats." He believed that becoming a healthy adult is necessarily tied to resolving the crisis of identity or suffering the feelings associated with role confusion.

Resolving this crisis successfully is complicated in Western cultures, given the mixed messages that society sends to gifted students. The messages can be so confusing that gifted students will engage in numerous behaviors to cope (Coleman & Cross, 2001). Some approaches include hiding or pretending to be what one is not. Other coping approaches include underachievement or other behaviors with potentially serious consequences.

Guiding the development of gifted children requires adults to work together to see that children successfully resolve the crises Erikson outlined in his eight stages of psychosocial development. Parents, teachers, and counselors should be aware that an individual gifted child could be affected by a psychosocial crisis at an earlier age than Erikson proposed. Adults should realize that some gifted children have an intellectual ability to understand the world years ahead of their chronological age, but have the emotional development typical of their same-age peers. To take full advantage of the explanatory power of Erikson's theory, one needs to interpret an individual gifted child's behaviors in light of this theory and the child's idiosyncratic development and personal characteristics. Armed with this information, adults are well prepared to help guide the psychological development of gifted children.

If Erikson was right that successful resolution of the psychosocial crises he outlined will result in gifted children leading their lives with feelings of hope, will, purpose, competence, fidelity, love, care, and wisdom, imagine what good can spring from well-adjusted, proactive, gifted adults.

FOR DISCUSSION

- Reflecting on Erikson's theory of psychosocial development and the asynchronous development of gifted children, describe behaviors of gifted children that may be explained by this theory.

- The importance of adults working to see that gifted students have ample opportunities to complete meaningful work successfully is noted. Discuss how you can provide such opportunities for the gifted children in your family or school.

CHAPTER 6

A Consideration of Axiomatic Statements

- Gifted and nongifted individuals share developmental characteristics.
- Gifted individuals have unique life experiences.
- Gifted individuals are impacted by external influences.

In this chapter, I would like to remind teachers, parents, and counselors of some of the most important influences on the psychological development of gifted students. With an awareness of these influences, adults can more effectively guide and nurture the development of these children in the social and emotional realms.

I hope to clarify these concepts with axiomatic, or self-evident, statements that illustrate many of the considerations in the life of a gifted student. Perhaps this will help you think of the ways in which gifted students are the same as others, different from others, and how they are impacted by outside influences.

Gifted Students Share Many Developmental Characteristics and Problems With All People

❖ Gifted students are children first; as such, they have much in common with children of average ability.
❖ People develop over time; therefore, as people, gifted students develop over time.

❖ Because talents manifest in numerous domains, children remain a very heterogeneous group of people; as children, few to no claims would be equally true for the entire group of gifted students.

❖ Every child grows up in a different environment; as children, gifted students grow up in different environments.

❖ People are agents in their own lives; as people, gifted students are agents in their own lives.

❖ Children vary in a multitude of personal characteristics; as children, gifted students vary in a multitude of personal characteristics.

❖ People need to feel accepted; as people, gifted students need to feel accepted.

❖ Knowledge is largely believed to be a construction of the person. As a subset of one's knowledge base, social cognition is developed idiosyncratically, through the eyes of an immature mind.

❖ Influencing the perceptions a person has about his or her life that were formed at an early age is often a difficult endeavor; as people, it is also difficult to influence the perceptions formed early in the lives of gifted students.

❖ Influences on the belief systems and behaviors of children begin with parents and continue with family members, but often are transcended by peer influence as the children get older, with the potential of significant others influencing them as they mature; as children, the same pattern is true for gifted students.

❖ A person's development is idiosyncratic, or particular to an individual or group; hence, patterns of development for gifted students will probably not closely reflect developmental milestones that are derived by averaging across groups of people.

❖ Environmental influences on a child can never transcend biologically based potential; as children, this is true for gifted students as well.

Gifted Students Have Life Experiences and Issues That Are Different Just Because They Are Gifted

❖ Because they have extraordinary capabilities, gifted students will likely experience certain aspects of the world differently from those who do not share the same gifts or talents.

❖ Giftedness is often experienced as feeling different from other students and, unlike other exceptionalities, can be hidden. Consequently, gifted students who act as agents in their own lives behave in compliance with their survival needs and social goals.

Influences Outside the Individual Have an Impact on Gifted Students

❖ Groups of people in society are treated differently relative to opportunities, expectations, and stereotypes; as people, gifted students' experiences will be affected by variables they cannot control.

❖ Definitions of giftedness change over time and vary in different societies. Whether or not children are thought to be gifted, how they are treated, and what subsequent perceptions and behaviors they engage in are variable and likely to be culturally relevant.

❖ Americans maintain numerous views of gifted students simultaneously. Gifted students receive mixed messages about their places in society, and that is often interpreted to be an indicator of the degree to which they are accepted and can be themselves.

❖ Schools tend to acknowledge and reward achievement over time (hence, labels such as *overachiever* are often given to gifted students to account for this prejudice for averaging achievement). Students of outstanding ability may be overlooked if their achievement is not consistent (if gifted students manifest enough extraordinary work to be noticed, but not enough to satisfy others, they are labeled *underachievers*).

❖ As gifted students get older, a primary task they have to complete in their psychological development is identity formation. Considering the axioms provided above, one could argue that the various, simultaneous, and often contradictory messages gifted students receive during their lives (when screened through perceptions that were developed when they were very young) destine gifted students to engage in numerous patterns of social coping behavior. These observed patterns may appear unreasonable or naïve to adults who have not experienced the world in the manner in which gifted students do. The challenge that teachers, parents, and counselors of gifted students must meet is to create learning environments in which gifted students feel fully accepted and to create environments that are also sophisticated in their approaches to developing the students' talents.

FOR DISCUSSION

- Which developmental characteristics are shared by gifted students and their nongifted peers?
- Which life experiences are unique to gifted students?
- What types of external influences affect gifted students?

CHAPTER 7

How Gifted Students Cope With Mixed Messages

- Stigma of Giftedness Paradigm
- Continuum of Visibility

In the previous chapter, I provided an overview of three categories of statements about the lives of gifted students that portrayed gifted students as existing within a world that sends them mixed messages that convey numerous unfavorable notions of the meaning of giftedness.

In this chapter, I am continuing the effort to illustrate how gifted students deal with these mixed messages. More specifically, I will relate what Larry Coleman and I have found to be a reasonable description of the experience of giftedness and how these students cope with life. From our research, we have posited that, for many gifted students, a figural aspect of the experience of giftedness is that they are often stigmatized, or thought to have certain identifying characteristics. Over the past 15 years, our research has shown time and again that this is an important component of the experience. In his book *Schooling the Gifted* (1985), Larry proposed a "Stigma of Giftedness Paradigm" that has three parts:

1. Gifted students want to have normal social interactions,
2. they believe that others will treat them differently if they learn of their giftedness, and

3. gifted students learn that they can manage information about themselves in ways that enable them to maintain greater social latitude.

Patterns of Gifted Students' Coping Behaviors

Given this set of beliefs, gifted students become active agents in trying to establish for themselves (against the backdrop of mixed messages) a degree and type of social latitude and experience that minimizes pain while allowing them to deal with the issues that change as they develop. Many of their strategies are rather obvious, while others are unspoken knowledge for them. The combined set of strategies was originally characterized on a continuum of visibility, with "Total Visibility" (playing a stereotypic role associated with being gifted in order to stand out from others) on one end, "Blending In" (finding ways to avoid standing out from the larger group of students) in the middle, and "Disidentifying" (proactively engaging in behavior opposite the group of which the gifted child might naturally be a part) at the other end.

For example, one student may choose to play the role of "mad scientist" to stand out as much as possible from others, while another chooses to navigate school along gender-typed expectations by diverting the energy associated with academic interests with what they perceive as more acceptable behaviors, such as dating or competing in athletics. Other types of coping behaviors include underachieving in school and more serious responses, like suicide. Typically, however, the coping behaviors of gifted students tend to be less harmful, sometimes evolving into behaviors that have some benefit to their academic performance, such as studying more and reading to escape their issues. Depending upon one's social goals, the behaviors of gifted students tend to fall into the categories listed on the continuum. With the exception of the "Total Visibility" category, the others reflect the students' desire to manage information. Consequently, their behaviors to that end are situation-specific; for example, not responding in school when a teacher asks a question ("Blending In"), or making friends with cliques of children in school whose reputation is opposite that of gifted students ("Disidentifying," e.g., becoming a "doper" instead of a "nerd").

My more recent research has caused me to add to the continuum a fourth position that reflects some students' most dire efforts at coping: taking one's own life. It fits the continuum notion in that the behaviors are coping efforts. It is different, however, in that I am unsure of the extent to which the coping is more connected with managing giftedness and its interrelatedness with larger life issues or merely an act most closely associated with depression and other correlates of suicide. We must concern ourselves, however, with the broader issue of the conditions in which gifted students live, what we as adults (teachers, counselors, parents) do to assist their development, and what we may unknowingly do to send them mixed messages. I believe that we need to take stock of our own beliefs about gifted students and seek additional training to prepare ourselves to assist in the development of all students.

The lives of gifted students are both the same as and quite different from other students' lives. Understanding the pain and suffering that children experience is only the beginning of what we, as the nurturers of gifted students, need to know. To minimize the mixed messages gifted students perceive, teachers, counselors, and parents must communicate expectations and beliefs held about giftedness. When they are congruent with each other, the messages the students perceive will be more similar, thus allowing them to thrive. When the messages are dissimilar, gifted students will engage in numerous coping behaviors, many of which are detrimental to their development and success as students. If you would like to read in greater detail about the lives of gifted students from my and Larry's perspective, then I encourage you to read any of the references listed below:

- ❖ Coleman, L. J. (1985). *Schooling the gifted*. New York, NY: Addison Wesley.
- ❖ Coleman, L. J., & Cross, T. L. (1988). Is being gifted a social handicap? *Journal for the Education of the Gifted, 11*, 41–56.
- ❖ Cross, T. L., Coleman, L. J., & Terhaar-Yonkers, M. (1991). The social cognition of gifted adolescents in schools: Managing the stigma of giftedness. *Journal for the Education of the Gifted, 15*, 44–55.

FOR DISCUSSION

- Name and discuss some of the mixed messages that gifted individuals receive.

- Are the mixed messages the same for gifted girls and gifted boys?

- How does the nature of these messages change over the life span?

- Reflect on an incident (as a parent, teacher, counselor) in which you unintentionally sent a mixed message to a gifted child. How would you handle a similar situation differently?

- What steps can you (as a parent, teacher, counselor) take to ensure that a gifted child does not engage in strategies that result in him or her "blending in" or becoming "invisible"?

CHAPTER 8

Examining Claims About Gifted Children and Suicide

KEY CONCEPTS

- Risk factors for adolescent suicide
- Paucity of research on gifted adolescent suicide

This chapter deals with a very sobering topic, one that appears too often in the newspapers, elicits strong opinions, and strikes fear in the hearts of parents: the suicides of gifted adolescents. In the following pages, I will provide an overview of what can and cannot be said on the topic based on actual research. I will focus my comments on gifted adolescents, even though preadolescents have died by their own hand. I will limit my comments to adolescents because they constitute by far the greater percentage of suicides (as compared to preteens) and because there is more information available on this age group. Please note the term *information*, rather than *data*. This distinction foreshadows the scarcity of research on the topic that will be discussed.

One characteristic of our culture is the growing rate of its population that commits suicide. Increases over the past decade are seen in virtually every age group, with the 15–24 age range showing significant increases. Suicide ranks as the second leading cause of death among young people (Capuzzi & Golden, 1988). One should note that adults older than 70 years have also shown large increases in their suicide rate over the past 20 years. Within the large group of school-aged children are subgroups that have a much higher rate of suicide than the rate for the entire group. For example, troubled adolescents have been estimated to attempt suicide at a rate of 33% (Tomlinson-Keasey & Keasey, 1988). From these studies, we can conclude that the rate of adolescent suicide has risen over the past decade, as have the rates of other groups. We also can conclude that subgroups vary in their rates of suicide.

A significant contribution of previous research on adolescent suicide has been the determination that there are significant risk factors:

◈ psychiatric disorders, such as depression and anxiety;
◈ drug and alcohol abuse;
◈ genetic factors;
◈ family loss or disruption;
◈ being a friend or family member of a suicide victim;
◈ homosexuality;
◈ rapid sociocultural change;
◈ media emphasis on suicide;
◈ impulsiveness and aggressiveness; and
◈ ready access to lethal methods. (Davidson & Linnoila, 1991)

One question I am often asked is whether the suicide rates of gifted adolescents differ significantly from the larger population of adolescents. In my own research, colleagues and I have conducted psychological autopsies of three gifted adolescents who committed suicide. In our research literature review, we found several interesting patterns.

The first pattern was the tendency for authors to make conclusions and recommendations about the incidence and nature of gifted suicide without supporting data. Moreover, general findings from marginally related studies were used to support the contention that the rate of suicide among gifted adolescents is the same as or lower than that of the larger population of adolescents. Again, these statements were based on no direct evidence.

The second pattern was the tendency of authors to cite each other's work based upon speculation. The net effect was the treatment of that speculation as concrete evidence. This pattern exists throughout research bodies and is not unique to this lore. What makes this research body different is that there is virtually no true research at the foundation of the base, yet truisms abound.

A third and more subtle pattern in the research was the tendency for authors to advocate for gifted children. Some of the pieces seemed less like efforts at research and more like efforts at protecting the image of gifted children.

Gifted Suicide Rates

Let me reiterate what was most often suggested in the literature: that the suicide rate of gifted adolescents is the same as or lower than that of the general population of adolescents. The basis for this claim is conceptual, not empirical. In fact, there is so little evidence available about gifted adolescents on this specific topic that nothing should be concluded. In other words, at this point, we cannot know.

Although seemingly an innocuous difference in assessments, the ramifications can vary significantly. For example, there are a growing number of academics considering the population of gifted adolescents in smaller, more representative subgroups than on an overall basis. In this case, students with differing characteristics might have markedly different incidences of suicide during adolescence. Some evidence for this claim can be found in research that has studied the lives of a large group of eminent people in the artistic and literary world. Among this subgroup, Ludwig (1995) found a higher incidence of suicide by the age of 30. He also found that "investigative types" (e.g., scientists) committed suicide at a higher rate than the general population after the age of 60.

I must interject a serious note of caution here. These data were drawn from a much older population, and, given the nature of the risk factors often associated with suicide, there may be a limited ability to generalize the findings. So, even though it stands to reason that subgroups of adolescents are at greater risk of committing suicide than other groups, there is not enough evidence to conclude whether or not gifted adolescents *per se* have a higher than average risk.

Some Reasons There Are Few Studies to Draw On

There are several reasons why there have been few studies conducted on the suicides of gifted students. A few include:

◆ the current data collected nationally about adolescent suicide do not include whether or not the individual was gifted,

◆ the varying definitions of giftedness and talent used across the United States make it difficult to know whether a child who committed suicide was gifted,

◆ issues of confidentiality limit access to data,

◆ conducting psychological autopsies of suicide victims is an expensive endeavor in terms of time and money,

◆ the fact that more adolescents than preadolescents commit suicide combined with the fact that secondary schools are not as actively engaged in identifying gifted students makes conducting research on this topic more difficult, and

◆ the terminal nature of suicide requires certain types of information to be garnered after the event.

Promising Studies

I am aware of a handful of studies that show promise of contributing to the research lore in significant ways. Two looked specifically at suicide ideation, one at the secondary level and one among honors students in college. A third study showing promise uses the psychological autopsies previously noted. Combined, these studies will add significantly to the current level of understanding.

One interesting question recognizing human variation within the gifted population deals with a topic of considerable debate among academics. That is, "What specific role, if any, do the qualities that some gifted adolescents possess play in their suicides?" For example, possible connections between gifted children's unusual sensitivities and perfectionism (Delisle, 1986) and isolationism and introversion (Kaiser & Berndt, 1985) with suicidal behavior have been raised. In the psychological autopsies being conducted, we have found that Piechowski's treatment of Dabrowski's theories has been helpful in interpreting the data collected. Some of the characteristics we have found beneficial in the data-analysis phase include intellectual-introspection, avid reading, curiosity, imaginational-fantasy, animistic and magical thinking, mixing truth and fiction, illusions, being emotional, strong affective memory, concern with death, depressive and suicidal moods, sensitivity in relationships, and feelings of inadequacy and inferiority (Piechowski, 1979).

What can we say about the suicides of gifted adolescents?

◈ Adolescents are committing suicide.

◈ Gifted adolescents are committing suicide.

◈ The rate of suicide has increased over the past decade for the general population of adolescents within the context of an overall increase across all age groups.

◈ It is reasonable to conclude that the incidence of suicide of gifted adolescents has increased over the past decade, while keeping in mind that there are no definitive data on the subject.

◈ Given the limited data available, we cannot ascertain whether the incidence of suicide among gifted adolescents is different from the incidence among the general population of adolescents.

FOR DISCUSSION

- How would you respond to this question: Are the suicide rates among gifted adolescents different than rates among nongifted adolescents?

- Reflect on and discuss the limitations associated with studying gifted adolescent suicide.

CHAPTER 9

On Chance and Being Gifted

KEY CONCEPTS

- Psychobiological influences
- Cultural influences
- Sociohistorical influences
- Family variables in context

Gifted students are the most diverse (heterogeneous) group of people to study because they can vary the most on the highest number of variables.

This chapter examines the role of chance in the lives of gifted students. More specifically, it illustrates how being gifted—whether or not one is identified as such—is affected by a particular chance factor. Specific examples are used to illustrate different manifestations of chance factors that affect the lives of gifted students. Because there are so many chance factors that potentially affect the psychological development of gifted students, I have sorted them into categories. For example, there are genetic, lifestyle, environmental, and overarching factors vs. instance, experiential, and coincidental chance factors.

The most obvious examples are the chance variables associated with the genetic makeup of a gifted child's parents. The point of noting this factor is to emphasize the sheer power of the psychobiological influence of the gifted child that is a function of the genetic makeup of the parents. Consequently, when children are born, they are not really clean slates; they have many predispositions, tendencies, and potentialities.

Another important chance factor is the location of a child's birth and upbringing. Imagine an intellectually gifted child born in Stockholm, Paris, Milledgeville, Moose Jaw, Trinidad, the Shoshoni and Arapaho Reservation, and so forth. Clearly, each location has significantly different histories and cultures. Hence, where gifted children happen to be born affects whether and how they might be identified as gifted and what their experiences will be.

When a gifted child is born is also quite significant. For example, imagine being a gifted student in science and math in the late 1950s in the United States. Because of the political uproar after the launch of Sputnik, great interest and money was put into gifted education in math and science. Now, imagine the same gifted child whose abilities were in language arts. Little interest existed at that time for those gifts.

Another example brings the topic closer to home. I call it "the family variables in context." Imagine a gifted girl, Jane, whose extraordinary skills are in the area of language arts. She lives in a medium-sized city in the United States. Her father is deceased, her mother works two full-time jobs at minimum wage to support the family, health care is not provided, and, at age 9, she is the oldest child and therefore often misses school to help care for the other children. All three children spend hours without adult supervision, and minimal books are available in the home.

Another gifted child, Tony, lives in a small rural community. He attends second grade in a school of 50 students in grades K–12. There are two teachers and one aide for the entire school. Tony's parents are ranchers on a small plot of land. The family has no television or computer. The boy's extraordinary abilities are in math.

Tony's new friend is a gifted boy named Juan whose parents are employed as migrant farm workers. They only live in Tony's farming community for about 2 months out of the year. At other times of the year, Juan's family moves across three other states. Juan likes Tony's town, partly because he gets to go to school there.

The last example of a gifted child is Brenda, a 16-year-old who is at the top of her school class. She is also an outstanding athlete. Both of her parents are well educated, and her father is a brilliant college professor. She has lived her life in a small college town and has grown up spending a great deal of time on the university campus. The family lives in a fine house with several computers and hundreds of books.

What is remarkable about the examples of Jane, Tony, Juan, and Brenda is that they are real people living in the same state—Wyoming—at the same time in history (names were changed to protect their anonymity). Implicit in using these life cases to illustrate different children with gifts and talents is the importance that chance factors play in the individual child's capacity to reach his or her potential. Given the information shared about these children, it is clear that their own potential and specific qualities *per se* have little to do with the likelihood of their reaching their potential. Rather, it is easy to see how chance factors have played a significant role in their lives to date. However, the fact that they were identified as gifted and were receiving (what I deemed to be) appropriate gifted education services creates hope for these students because it means that the myriad forms of variation in conditions and types of abilities that have been described were still understandable to professional educators working in Wyoming schools. So, while genetic makeup cannot be transcended, it does not have to create insurmountable hurdles to identifying and serving gifted students. We merely need to remind ourselves that our science and pedagogy must emanate from the idea that gifted students are the most diverse group of people to study because their characteristics vary on the most number of variables. The fact that chance exists in so many ways means that the training of school personnel must recognize and attend to these factors.

One of the most powerful chance factors affecting gifted children is the socioeconomic status (SES) of their parents. The research on SES and achievement is clear: There are certain factors of poverty that mitigate against school success. I contend that the achievement gap between what is possible and what is actually accomplished among our gifted students from the poorest families is the greatest of any group of students. Although everyone can agree that all students should be expected to reach their potential, gifted students from the lowest SES are at the greatest risk for underachievement. And, as the brief case descriptions of a small number of gifted students in Wyoming illustrate, the poor gifted child, although quite diverse in background and circumstances, can be identified and serviced.

Why were teachers in the schools in Wyoming able to meet the needs of the gifted students described above? The state struggles with severe financial swings in its economy, which affect its schools. It is a largely rural state with many one-room schools remaining. Many years ago, when I served as president of the Wyoming Association for Gifted Education (WAGE), it was clear that the state's school districts had differing definitions of giftedness, and programs were often created, lived, thrived, and ended on the basis of an individual teacher's work. I participated in numerous discussions with long-term teachers of the gifted who revealed many of the same difficulties most states experience today. For example, they described feeling alone in their commitment to gifted students; that there was not enough money to work on behalf of gifted students and too little general support provided by administrators; that the state department did not emphasize gifted education enough; that they did not have enough resources; and that, because there was only one university in the state to provide training, too little training was available to them. Even with all of these potential limitations, the teachers were able to identify the various manifestations of giftedness, understand the other chance factors that affected gifted students' abilities to reach their potential, and then create learning conditions that were appropriate and beneficial.

I believe some intangible factors that exist in the unique state of Wyoming are important in understanding why the teachers were so successful. The state was settled by independent people who endured certain hardships to live there. I also think that the state's history of accommodating vast differences among its students is due to the degree of rurality of the state and its history of one-room schools. These factors created a mindset that "teaching to the needs of each child" must be the rule, rather than the exception. Therefore, some of the tenets of differentiation existed in Wyoming long before the recent resurgence of the concept.

The field of gifted education has evolved over the years to the point where many advocate a gifted services model, rather than a specific programmatic model. The former has the advantage of being able to attend to the individual needs of students as compared to the latter example, which generally requires identification approaches that match a type of gifted student to a typically narrowly conceived program. An ongoing problem with the programmatic model is the inherent limitations of schools not having enough programs to accommodate all gifted students. In small schools, a critical mass of students has proven to limit specific programs that are offered. This evolution lends itself to schools being better suited to deal with the diversity that gifted students manifest, including their chance variables. Assuming attention is paid to the goal of accommodating all needs of gifted students in school, then Jane's, Tony's, Juan's, and Brenda's needs all can be met. Allegiance to programs is not the same as allegiance to students. The first step school personnel need to take is to accept the challenge of meeting all of the needs of all gifted students. Secondly, educators need to understand fully the diversity of giftedness. The third step is to be able to identify as many chance factors as possible, separating those that are to the advantage of the gifted student from the ones that cannot be dealt with. To accomplish this, the child's psychological development will need to be considered in a sophisticated manner. A planned set of services that draw on any necessary resources available to the teacher will become the tools of the trade. In other words, the classroom becomes the home base, not the student's entire world.

Imagine the scope of benefits we can bring to the lives of students with gifts and talents by reducing any negative effects that chance factors play in their lives.

FOR DISCUSSION

- The influence of the Sputnik launch on gifted education was mentioned. Discuss other sociohistorical events and their influence on gifted education.

- Which of the following chance factors do you consider to be the most influential on the development of a gifted child: psychobiological, cultural, sociohistorical, or parents' socioeconomic status? Explain why.

Being Gifted Is Abnormal?

by Laurence J. Coleman

Much of the confusion among parents about how to deal with their child who may be gifted or is gifted is connected to misunderstanding about the meaning of normal or its dreaded opposite, abnormal. My intent in this essay is to provide some clarification about this idea as a means to reframe superstitious thinking about several issues that seem to be distorted by an incomplete understanding of normal.

An Interpretation of the Meaning of Normal

If there is such a condition or state of being called "normal," what is it? Normal means something is common and happens with regularity; and it is the arithmetic average or some other indicator of central tendency. But, normal is something more. Basically, normal refers to the normal curve, which is a bell-shaped graph, by which people can be ordered from less to more of a particular characteristic, such as height or intelligence. The highest point of the bell represents the most number of people, such that the average is at that point, and as the bell slopes symmetrically downward, there are fewer and fewer people at the extremes. In terms of intellectual ability, children may fall under this curve from the relatively few cognitively disabled at one end to the most populous middle to the few intellectually advantaged at the other. It is as normal for someone to be at the low end as in the middle or the high end. Thus, one may be above or below average, but one is also normal in terms of the fact that everyone falls under this umbrella.

When the popular press describes normal child development, the descriptions have children mastering significant developmental tasks, such as walking, speaking, drawing, and so forth. These tasks, often called milestones or markers, are linked to accomplishments associated with chronological ages like 9 months or 10 years. Milestones are easier to see when children are young, as in the case of walking or talking. More subtle markers, such as understanding gravity or logical reasoning, later use age/grade equivalents.

The impression is that normal is the same as doing certain tasks at specific times. This conventional interpretation distorts some significant facts. First, those times are not precise points, but really are broad bands of overlapping moments representing a sequence of points across time. One task follows another, but the interval between markers is not uniform. This is the normal pattern. Secondly, the milestones represent development in universal areas, which means all children attain them spontaneously at varying rates and ages. Some children take so long to meet a milestone, as in the case of some cognitively disabled children, that they do not seem to meet them; and others, as in the case of some gifted children, advance so rapidly to adult levels that it appears they skip markers. Reaching a single marker means little by itself. A slow or fast pattern becomes apparent over a series of tasks. It is normal for some children to be fast and others less so. For gifted children faster is the defining developmental pattern. Rapid development is normal development when it applies to these universal tasks.

Concurrent with universal areas of development, and with some coincidental overlapping, are field-specific areas of development. Common examples are playing the piano, doing mathematics, reading texts, drawing, chess, swimming, and astrophysics. These have been aptly named nonuniversal domains by Feldman because most children could attain, but relatively few do, advanced levels of development. Children develop in these areas because of circumstance, luck, and their own intention. Unlike universal development where children spontaneously develop to more advanced levels, for nonuniversal domains children have to have the opportunity and the desire to develop to the high levels of these areas. (There appears to be one group of children, prodigies, who might have a natural advantage in particular fields.) Nonuniversal markers of development are peculiar to a field or domain and are significantly relatively independent of chronological age. Therefore, the conventional age markers of universal domains make little sense in nonuniversal fields. Normal continues to refer to the sequence of development, but the sequence in a field is embedded and regulated by the inherent structure of that field and the efforts of the child to master that field. In nonuniversal domains, a young person can be doing adult level tasks. As one proceeds to master a field, one is behaving normally.

I use this discussion to emphasize the fact that normal refers to development in universal and nonuniversal areas. It is normal to develop at varying rates to reach higher levels. In universal domains, everyone happens to do it and that is normal. In nonuniversal domains, some people develop to the highest level and that, too, is normal in that specific field. In essence, I have been making the case that rapid development and much of the behavior of gifted children makes better sense as expressions of normality, universal and nonuniversal, than as instances of abnormality. Although it is not the conventional belief, if a child is functioning at a level higher than her peers, she is behaving normally, not abnormally.

The Pervasiveness of the Beliefs Linked to Conceptions of Normal

The misunderstanding of the meaning of normal infects how people think about gifted children. The situation becomes apparent in the stability of certain beliefs about children who are gifted.

Pushiness and Rapid Development

Recognition of the presence of advanced development, or preco-ciousness, elicits presumptive reactions in many people. Seeing a child behaving and acting like an older child elicits the deduction that the parents have pushed the child. The underlying core belief is that rapid development is unnatural and abnormal. Someone must be pushing the child beyond his age-mates. The fact that a child generates much of the "push" seems counterintuitive, even though research with children and parents confirm that the children have not been pushed toward higher achievement. The idea that a gifted child is like a hurricane, gathering energy and resources from the environment to grow, seems implausible; yet, that is the case. The pervasiveness of this belief about "pushy parents" is evident from often-repeated statements from other parents, from educators in general, and, even more surprisingly, from teachers in special programs for the gifted. The misguided belief is so ingrained that changing the belief about pushiness is almost insurmountable. I cannot explain this resistance.

Superstitious Thinking About "Mental" Health

Worrying about a child's mental health is rooted in the idea of normal and the fear of a child being abnormal. Common associated beliefs are:

◈ having lots of friends is a better than having few friends,
◈ engaging in solitary interests and activities is a sign of potential problems,
◈ feeling different is a precursor to maladjustment, and
◈ being well rounded and balanced is a sure sign of good social-emotional health.

The statements are often translated as the idea that it is dangerous to have few friends, to be socially disinterested, to like being alone, to have singular strengths, and to feel different from peers.

The belief that having many friends for most children is normal and desirable does not match the way friendships are distributed in groups. Friendship is not evenly distributed. Some children get many choices for friends from their peers; the rest receive less; and some even receive no choices. This pattern is normal. The lack of choice is not negative by itself. It is the interpretation by the child of the friendship patterns he or she can choose from that is important to understand. The child's concern with the friendships he or she makes is the issue, not the adult's.

The belief that being solitary is a sign of dysfunction is another overgeneralization. Not everyone is interested in having lots of friends. Being socially disinterested is normal, too. Some children may have interests that lead to their being more solitary than other children. Abstract specialized interests, either literary or scientific, can lead one to spend time with one's own thoughts. If there are no others with your interest, the consequence is being alone or giving up the interest. Being solitary, and even feeling alone, is not uncommon when one has specialized interests beyond conventional age-mates and/or one is working on complex problems beyond others' understanding at that time. It is not until adulthood that some children find peers.

Feeling different is common among children who are gifted. It is normal and not an automatic sign of future social-emotional problems. Feeling different shows that the stigma of giftedness is real to some children. Learning to deal with the differentness is a condition of life for gifted children. Learning how to be different and still be true to oneself is a real question. Forming one's identity and managing one's identity as a person who is gifted and talented is not an easy task. It is easier for those who are athletically gifted than those who have more cognitive abstract interests. The social context in which the child lives and learns can lessen these feelings.

Well-roundedness is not a sure sign of mental health. Being out of balance is close to the natural state of gifted children. Uneven development is normal for gifted children. The more extreme is the advanced development, the greater lack of well-roundedness. The more esoteric the field of interest, the less well-rounded the child may be. Rapid development and intense interests beyond one's chronological age bring strain to the individual and to the family. This strain has to be acknowledged and discussed. There is no evidence to suggest that parents of gifted children should fear the appearance of severe emotional problems more than parents of their nongifted peers.

Children Also Have Thoughts About What Normal Means for Being Gifted

The connection between ability and accomplishment in many children's minds is mistaken. The belief is this: Having to work hard on something means you are *not* gifted. Accomplishment and excellence always require hard work and commitment. Working hard is a prerequisite for being excellent or a top performer. Where that belief originated I do not know, but it is completely inaccurate.

In this essay I have attempted to build a broader understanding of the concept of normal. I have made the case that gifted children are normal children. I have suggested that keeping this idea in mind can help us understand some of the superstitious thinking connected with giftedness. Again, there is no evidence to suggest that parents of gifted children should fear the appearance of severe emotional problems more than parents of their nongifted peers.

Emotions and Giftedness

by Sal Mendaglio

More than 30 years of counseling experience supports the proposition that emotion is a primary force in human experience. Further evidence can be found in recent theory and research. The popularity of emotional intelligence (Salovey & Mayer, 1990), with its emphasis on emotion awareness and communication, acknowledges the importance of emotions. Research in personality suggests that emotions contribute significantly to the development of personality (Izard & Ackerman, 2000). In Dabrowski's theory of positive disintegration, an influential theory in our field, emotions direct the course of human development (Mendaglio, 2008). As a result of this evidence, I have made emotion a central component in the model that I have constructed to guide my work with gifted individuals of all ages.

In the affective cognitive model of giftedness (Mendaglio, 2007), helping individuals to understand emotions and how to effectively handle them form integral parts of the counseling process. My conceptualization of emotion in gifted individuals reflects a fundamental assumption regarding giftedness, namely that gifted individuals share much in common with all other individuals. From this perspective, my task becomes twofold. First, I need to select principles from the pool of established psychological principles that have the potential to explain human experience. Second, I must transform those principles by viewing them through the lens of characteristics that differentiate gifted individuals. In the case of emotions, I have drawn on principles based on the cognitive theory of emotion and have adapted them by using characteristics associated with giftedness.

The cognitive theory of emotion is a widely accepted approach to the psychology of emotion. This theory states that we create our emotions by our interpretation of events. In general, we interpret a situation and, based on how we interpret it, we may or may not experience an emotion. The interpretation component is key and can be seen as our responding to the question: What, if anything, does this situation have to do with my well-being? If our answer is that it has no bearing on our well-being, there is no emotion. If, on the other hand, we interpret the situation as threatening to our well-being, we experience negative emotions. When we deem the situation to enhance our well-being, we experience positive emotions. Situations that spark the process may be real or imaginary. We may have an encounter with a partner and interpret his or her comments as critical and then experience irritation or anger. Our partner may insist that the utterance was simply an observation and no criticism was intended, but we remain adamant in our interpretation and the emotion is created and persists. Or, we may think of a demanding task that we are to do in the future; for example, a student may think of an upcoming test or a professional may think of an upcoming presentation, and, depending on their interpretations, negative or positive emotions may be created. If the student and professional believe that they are unprepared for the tasks, both will feel anxiety. If they feel prepared, they may see the future task as an opportunity to shine and feel pleased at this thought. The cognitive theory of emotion has become quite entrenched in certain forms of counseling and psychotherapy and in the theoretical underpinnings of psychological stress. Rational emotive psychotherapy has long proposed that it is not the events that cause us distress, but our interpretation of them. In the area of stress, the notion that stress is in the eye of the beholder has long been accepted.

In the cognitive theory of emotion, then, interpretation is the key to understanding how emotions arise. Interpretation is a cognitive process and thereby is affected by cognitive ability. Although other factors impinge on our interpretation of situations, such as self-esteem related to the situation or event or our memory of our handling such events in the past, I assume that the level of cognitive ability or intelligence is an important factor in interpretation. As the level of intelligence increases, the quantity of information gleaned and speed of processing increases. Speed of processing does not guarantee accuracy. High intelligence enables us to process a great deal of information quickly, but we may arrive at an interpretation of events that does not reflect another person's intended message or the reality of the situation. However, rapid processing may account for the rapid rise and fall of emotions in gifted youth often reported by parents in counseling sessions.

In my conception of giftedness, a high level of intelligence produces heightened sensitivity, a characteristic often attributed to giftedness. In my model, awareness is a synonym for sensitivity. Advanced intelligence enables an individual to be aware of, for example, nuances of interpersonal interactions. Such heightened awareness has given rise to the saying: Gifted individuals feel more because they see more. In my opinion, this is not equated with value—gifted individuals are no more valuable than any other human being—but feeling more and seeing more are accounted for by the cognitive theory of emotions. Advanced intellectual ability causes the gifted individual to perceive more information during his interactions, and this affects the intensity of the emotions created: more information perceived, more grist for the interpretation mill. This applies to both negative and positive emotions.

This blending of psychological principles and characteristics of gifted individuals leads to strategies aimed at dealing with emotion expression by gifted individuals. A common response to emotions generally can be described as attempts to "fix" emotions or to "rescue" the person. Often this takes the form of using logic in an attempt to reason with the emotional individual, to show, for example, how unreasonable or silly it is to feel that badly about the event. I think that all of us have experienced how ineffective such approaches are. In fact, we may unwittingly throw fuel into the fire as we attempt to convince the person of the folly of his interpretations. Further, we know from our experience with emotions that it is difficult to be rational in the heat of the moment, but we typically persist in using logic in the face of others' expressions of emotion. From my perspective, gifted individuals will use their intelligence to cling on to their interpretation of events, while finding errors in others' reasoning. One strategy that flows from my analysis of emotion is that we should avoid reasoning with the emotional person, and instead we should offer a sympathetic and, perhaps, empathetic reaction, staying well away from challenging his interpretation of events. A sympathetic, nonjudgmental ear will contribute to the individual's ability to restore his equilibrium. Reasoning, logic, and problem solving—all of which impinge on the interpretation component—will likely be more effective once the emotion has dissipated.

Intense emotionality is often associated with giftedness. In my view, an explanation of emotions experienced and expressed by gifted individuals is achieved by blending established psychological knowledge regarding emotion and characteristics of gifted individuals. In my work with gifted individuals, providing them with a coherent integration of the cognitive theory of emotions and heightened sensitivity has proven useful in helping gifted individuals understand emotions in themselves and others.

Negotiating the Vicissitudes of Chance Factors

by Rena Subotnik

In 1983, Abraham Tannenbaum published his masterpiece, *Gifted Children: Psychological and Educational Perspectives*. In it he proposed a model of five factors (general ability, special abilities, nonintellective facilitators, environmental influences, and chance factors) involved with fulfilling the promise of giftedness. Four of the five components overlap with those proposed in the 1970s and '80s by other greats in our field (e.g., Joseph Renzulli, Robert Sternberg, David Feldman, and Benjamin Bloom). One factor was featured explicitly and exclusively by Tannenbaum—recognition of the role of chance.

Tannenbaum cited the work of Austin (1978) in his discussion of chance factors. One of Austin's typologies includes being in the right place at the right time (and prepared). A second type involves "stirring up a pot of random ideas" (Tannenbaum, 1983, p. 206), trying to increase the likelihood that some new experiences or connections will emerge from these efforts. A third type of chance factor is exemplified by Alexander Fleming's discovery of penicillin. In this case, a chance experience connects in your mind to something you have been working on and leads to a new insight.

Chance factors play a bigger role during some life and career stages than others. Tannenbaum (1983) pointed out that the school years are far less surprising than the world outside of school. In spite of schooling's predictability, however, there are still many opportunities for the hand of fate to disrupt smooth passage through grade levels and academic expectations. I would argue that psychologists, educators, coaches, and counselors have a role to play in helping young people negotiate the vicissitudes of chance factors during the school years. Further, the lessons learned in the process can later be applied to negotiating career and personal life trajectories.

From my understanding of Tannenbaum's (1983) discussion of chance factors, they can be actively sought or avoided. For example, suppose one of your students is sorely disappointed because she did not win a part that she had auditioned for in the school play. While she prepares for a less desirable part, she could be encouraged to practice as an understudy for the part she wanted. Such preparation would demonstrate to the director her great commitment to the play's success, and may lead to an opportunity should the performer of choice not be available for some unexpected reason.

Alternatively, it's very possible that a student may be assigned to a weak teacher in a subject that the student later hopes to major in. If there is no recourse to the assignment, then the student can be guided to consider some out-of-school mentoring in the subject, a program of reading, or an online course to compensate for the teacher's lack of expertise or skill.

Chance factors also can be passively received or rejected. Suppose one of your students had been hoping for an internship opportunity. At a volleyball game he happens to meet the parent of one of his classmates. This parent is a professional in the area of his interest. The student could grab the opportunity and promote a potential internship for himself or let the opportunity go. Too many young people lack self-confidence, or they feel they are not really agents of their own destiny. Without our guidance they may not capitalize on chance meetings, or feel they can take an opportunity unless it is offered directly.

In the late 1990s, Franz Mönks asked me to get some information about admission to the Juilliard School's precollege program for one of his clients. Franz was hoping to avoid being put on hold from Europe and then end up not talking to the right person. Hunter College, where I was professor at the time, was a cross-town bus trip away from the Juilliard School. The director of admissions, Mary Gray, made an appointment with me to come see her. It turned out, *serendipitously*, that Mary had a 3-year-old daughter, and Mary was very interested in hearing about Hunter College Elementary School. We talked at length about issues associated with selective programs for children and developed a deep bond that has lasted until today (although she no longer works at Juilliard).

Mary's descriptions of conservatory education intrigued me, and I proposed a study to her that she presented successfully to the president of Juilliard. The study ended up lasting about 4 years, much of it conducted in collaboration with Linda Jarvin. We explored the non-intellective, nonmusical components of conservatory education, not only at Juilliard, but also at the New England Conservatory and the Curtis Institute. We came up with a model of talent development that included variables that were associated with success by students, educators, and gatekeepers in the classical music world (Subotnik & Jarvin, 2005). Some of those variables address chance events—learning to be receptive to instruction (or challenging it in a "tasteful" manner), persistence in good and bad times, self-promotion, social skills, restoring lost self-confidence, and strategic risk taking. Rather than assuming that these skills are natural to some people and not to others, conservatory education explicitly seeks to improve the skills of those for whom the psychosocial dimensions of their lives are underdeveloped.

My passion is to see this, what I call "psychological strength training," be available to gifted students in academic settings. With a fully implemented program, or even some occasional boosters, the chance opportunity or setback can be greeted by young people with grace and creativity.

SECTION 2

Guiding Gifted Children

Once we know a little about who gifted children are, it is important for us to use that knowledge to help them function successfully in their environment.

This section opens with two special commentary pieces meant to do just that—help parents and teachers lead gifted children to success in their environments. First is a discussion of how parents and other family members can influence gifted students and facilitate their success by Paula Olszewski-Kubilius. Mary Ann Swiatek then offers a discussion of acceleration issues, noting her own personal experiences as a gifted child.

The first three chapters—"Guiding and Supporting the Development of Gifted Children," "Practical Advice for Guiding the Gifted," and "Working on Behalf of Gifted Students"—offer ideas about things teachers, parents, and counselors should consider, and some specific things they can do for their young charges. I allude to the important role of communication in many of the suggestions listed in these first three chapters, and, in the fourth, "Developing Relationships, Communication, and Identity," I focus on how it can be a difficult aspect of childhood. Communicating with the adults in their lives, building relationships with other children, and developing their own sense of identity are all aspects of childhood that can be traumatic or relatively easy. This chapter gives some suggestions for smoothing the pathway for gifted children.

The fifth chapter of this section discusses a new perspective on teaching students in what I have titled "Swagger or Humility or

Swagger and Humility: A New Goal for Educating Students With Gifts and Talents." Following that, in the chapter entitled "Putting the Well-Being of All Students (Including Gifted Students) First," I explore the concept of well-being and what this means for gifted students in the school context.

The next three chapters look at issues affecting students in school on a more personal level. "Owning the Problem of Undesirable Behavior: Disintermediation and How Our Children Are Taught to Drink, Smoke, and Gamble," looks at how children are influenced by society's messages about acceptable behaviors. The next chapter, "Self-Mutilation and Gifted Children," discusses an interesting and harmful behavior of many adolescents today, cutting, and the psychological reasons behind some students' preoccupation with such a dangerous behavior. This section also revisits the previous conversation about suicide among gifted students in "On Preventing Suicide Among Gifted Students."

Finally, in "Gifted Students and the Adults Who Provide for Them: Lessons Learned From Terrorism," I examine the reactions and coping strategies of the academically gifted adolescents at the Indiana Academy for Science, Mathematics, and Humanities following the September 11, 2001, terrorist attacks. I then discuss the lessons learned from this tragedy in relation to guiding the social and emotional development of gifted students.

How Families Can Facilitate Students' Success

by Paula Olszewski-Kubilius

The most important influence on a developing child is the family. Those of us who are parents or work with children know this and often feel overwhelmed about the responsibility, particularly regarding a child with exceptional needs, such as a gifted child. One of the roles of parents (and teachers) is finding out about and providing good educational opportunities for talented children. However, the more important role for parents is shaping and influencing the personalities, beliefs, values, and motivation of their children because these ultimately determine success, achievement, and happiness. Successful people are those who are open to possibilities, embrace challenges, take risks, are resilient after failures, and are willing to work harder than anyone else. There are no guidelines regarding raising a child, particularly a gifted child, and there is great diversity among the families of high achieving and creative adults. So, does the research on the development of gifted individuals have anything to guide parents in their efforts? I believe it does.

One critical factor in the fruition of talent is beliefs about the nature of abilities and talents. Research has shown that these beliefs will determine both how you approach learning and how you deal with challenges, setbacks, competition, and failure. No successful person is without failures nor has succeeded without being challenged. The most eminent individuals had setbacks and failures. So, the issue is not if, or even when or how often, one will fail, but what one's reaction will be.

Carol Dweck (2008) has identified two "mindsets" or sets of beliefs about ability that have profound implications for children's achievement. One is the belief that ability is something a person is born with—a fixed amount that determines how smart and ultimately how successful one can be. A second mindset is focused on learning and growth and includes a perspective that ability is something that changes and develops, particularly with work and study. Individuals who subscribe to a "fixed" mindset often avoid challenging learning situations because they view them as "tests" of their ability rather than as opportunities for learning, and they fear failing those tests. Often, they suffer from performance anxiety. These individuals devalue the role of effort in success and achievement and believe that only effortless achievement is an indication of talent or giftedness. Students with a fixed mindset begin to flounder when work in school gets more difficult because having to expend more effort to get the same good grades means they are not that gifted. Some students with a fixed mindset might simply stop trying to do well in school altogether, rejecting any situation they perceive as an assessment of their ability or an attempt by an adult to "measure" it. They may complain that school is boring to deflect parents and teachers away from their fear of failure.

Persons who have a "growth" mindset typically approach challenging academic situations as opportunities to learn and improve. They embrace rather than fear them. They react to setbacks such as poor grades with increased effort, problem solving, and planning. They turn failures into motivating, energizing opportunities. They believe in their capacity to learn and do not feel they have to prove themselves over and over again. They feel they are at their best when they are learning and improving, not when they get good grades or test scores.

We want children to have a growth mindset, yet inadvertently, parents and educators in gifted education promote the opposite. We do this by expecting perfect grades and being overly critical of students for mistakes. As parents or teachers, we say things such as "How can you be gifted and yet not know this?" Or "How could such a smart kid like you make such a mistake?" We praise children for being smart, for learning quickly, and for effortless achievement, rather than for improvement, willingness to take on a challenge, resiliency, or hard work. We make comparisons between children and we peg them into categories such as "the smart one" or "the athletic one" or "the musical one." We set (and lower) our expectations regarding a child's achievement based on her IQ score or test grades. We create gifted programs based on a single test score with little opportunity for children to "learn or earn" their way into it. All of these contribute to the perpetuation of the potentially debilitating belief that ability and talent are some measurable entities that predetermine success.

How can parents and educators facilitate the development of a growth mindset? According to Dweck (2008), parents and teachers can do a lot to help children develop beliefs and attitudes that support achievement, generate motivation, and promote lifelong learning simply by being aware and careful of their verbal messages and their reactions to children.

For example, Dweck (2008) recommended that parents and teachers be careful about using the term *gifted* with children and specifically labeling them as such. Although a parent may be proud that a child is in a gifted program, emphasize instead that such a placement is simply a response to her current learning needs so as to provide the challenge necessary to promote further growth and development. Stress that your family is interested in learning more than performance and that you will tolerate less than perfect grades. View report cards and grades as feedback and opportunities to assess individual progress and set new goals. Learn what your child's interests and talents are and encourage her to pursue and excel in those areas, while not expecting high performance in all subjects or activities.

Talk explicitly to children about individual differences and how people learn and grow at different rates, and therefore need different kinds of programs or classes at different times. Avoid comparisons between children and instead, compare a child's current performance to his previous one. Help children set learning goals rather than performance goals. React calmly when a child falters or fails, helping him to view poor grades or scores as indications that a different approach or more effort is needed. Parents should model behaviors such as risk taking, challenge seeking, asking for help, persevering despite less than optimal performance, and resiliency after failure.

Create multifaceted *services* for gifted children that address their learning and psychological needs rather than *programs* to slot them into. Develop understanding among teachers that being gifted does not mean perfect grades and high performance at all times in all subjects. Encourage a perspective on giftedness that recognizes domain-specific talent rather than general ability or IQ. Reward and model risk taking, perseverance, and growth, as well as performance.

Acceleration

by Mary Ann Swiatek

Let me tell you some things about my background that don't show up in my bio. I was reading before I entered kindergarten. The principal of my school advised my parents to refuse if anyone ever suggested that I skip a grade. He warned them that grade skipping was bad for children. My advanced reading remained a problem until I reached high school. My school never could decide how to address it and, as a result, I was subject accelerated some years and not others. I did reading classes at some grade levels multiple times (memorably, I had to use the same fourth-grade reader in both third and fourth grade), and at other grade levels not at all. As a college student, I did an independent library research project to explore whether grade skipping really was "bad for children." To my surprise, I learned that acceleration has strong research support. In graduate school, I was fortunate to work with Dr. Camilla Benbow, who authored several of the studies I had read. Under her direction, I was able to contribute to the research on acceleration. In fact, the first journal article I ever authored was on that topic. My own research also showed that acceleration worked. Material was learned rapidly and well, and students enjoyed the challenge and looked back on their acceleration with satisfaction even years later.

In the years since graduate school, I have become involved with my state organization for the education of the gifted. As a member of their speakers' bureau, I do presentations for parent groups, in-services for teachers, and conference presentations on a number of topics. The most requested topic is acceleration. On one hand, it's frustrating to be asked the same questions about acceleration over and over again. On the other hand, it's good to see that people are asking what the research says about acceleration. Clearly, if such questions were not being asked and answered, acceleration would be used even less frequently than it is now. People seem to fear that accelerating gifted children will kill their grade-point averages, weaken the foundation of their learning, destroy their confidence, exhaust them mentally, and/or ruin their social lives. In the past, these worries aggravated me, and even made me angry. With time, I've come to better understand their sources. It seems to me that there are three main reasons why people get nervous when they hear the word *acceleration*.

First, people understand that experiencing success helps children develop self-confidence and self-esteem—which is true. What people often do not understand, however, is that experiencing success without first doing a reasonable amount of work is far less powerful and positive than experiencing success as a payoff for effort. A child who succeeds without ever really trying may develop confidence, but it can be a shaky confidence that crumbles when a real challenge is faced. Further, without ever having the need for it, that individual may fail to develop a good work ethic, perseverance, study skills, and other characteristics and abilities that are necessary for dealing with challenging situations when they do arise. The struggle that ensues can convince the person that he or she never was really gifted at all—so much for confidence and self-esteem.

Second, many people believe that what is *accelerated* in acceleration is the student—that is, the student is "pushed." This belief contributes to many fears, including that acceleration will lead to poor academic achievement, burnout, and even social difficulties. In actuality, however, acceleration properly implemented is about pushing the curriculum to keep up with the student, not the other way around. One must begin by understanding that gifted students learn quickly, with fewer repetitions than typical students require. Sometimes they even reason things out without formal instruction. Repetitive worksheets and homework that are designed to help typical students learn are excessive and unnecessary for gifted learners. Similarly, although it may be true that teaching others helps the teacher learn, this works only if the teacher has something left to learn. Once material is mastered, repeating it by drilling, practicing, or teaching others is not useful. An accurate view of acceleration, in which the student pushes the curriculum to keep up with his or her learning needs, precludes concerns about poor achievement and burnout.

Third, people often worry that an accelerated student will never be able to fit in socially with chronologically older students. The difference in age between an accelerated student and his or her classmates often is not as large as one might assume, however. Students who are relatively old for their grades before acceleration will not be much younger than the youngest students already in the new class. It also is important to understand that gifted students as a group are not socially backward, as some may believe; many are advanced socially, as well as intellectually. The nature of friendship is another important consideration. Most friendships are based on some point of similarity between the individuals involved. When acceleration is correctly used, it places gifted students with classmates who are more similar to them than their age-mates in terms of how they think and what they know. Such points of similarity can facilitate the development of friendships.

Overall, worries about accelerating a gifted student often seem related to both a failure to keep in mind the unique characteristics of gifted students and a misunderstanding of the ways in which gifted students are just like everyone else. Gifted students' ability to learn quickly without much repetition and their advanced ways of thinking make them unique and well suited to a faster pace and higher level of study than are typical for their age. Like everyone else, they develop true self-esteem and confidence by exerting reasonable effort to achieve meaningful success, and they are most likely to develop real friendships with people with whom they share something in common. Keeping these points in mind helps explain why research has shown that, when used judiciously and with appropriate students, acceleration is not "bad for children," but quite the opposite.

CHAPTER 10

Guiding and Supporting the Development of Gifted Children

KEY CONCEPTS

- Strategies exist for guiding and supporting gifted students.
- Adults' best efforts cannot prevent struggles and emotional turmoil from occurring in a child's life.
- A gifted child is a child first.
- Communication among groups of adults is vital.
- Try to understand the social milieu of the school.
- Serve as a clearinghouse for information about gifted students.
- Learn about the gifted child's personality and social goals.
- Teach the child to better understand him- or herself.
- Provide opportunities for gifted children to be together.

Having spent several years conducting research, working directly with gifted students in various roles, and reading others' studies on the topic of the social and emotional needs of gifted students, I have come to believe there are several strategies that will help parents, teachers, and counselors guide gifted children.

Some of the topics have a substantial research base, some have only a modest research base, and some have little to no published research base supporting them. Cutting across these ideas is a form of conventional wisdom I have seen expressed by many in the field. I suspect the reason such widespread conventional wisdom exists is primarily because our professional experiences become our primary source of data as we try to make sense of the world. Although I believe there is danger in relying too much on personal experiences when making generalizations, I do respect the fact that drawing on multiple forms of data is an appropriate method for making informed decisions. So, to break with my past practice of trying to forward only those ideas that have emerged from published research findings, I am going to provide a partial list of ideas I believe have merit when trying to guide gifted children.

I will let my qualifiers reflect the degree of confidence that I have in these ideas. Some are speculative, while research soundly supports others. Some are taken from research in gifted education, some come from outside the field, and some come largely from my own professional experience. Consider these ideas for use by parents, teachers, and counselors who guide the social and emotional development of gifted children:

1. Realize that your best efforts cannot prevent struggles and emotional turmoil from occurring in the child's life. Your efforts may, however, allow the child to effectively transcend the difficulties associated with youth, particularly those issues unique to gifted children.

2. Remember that the gifted child is a child first. Adults often forget that the young person they are dealing with is, in fact, a child. When listening to gifted children talk about academic topics, it is difficult to remember they are very likely at the same general social and emotional development level as their nongifted peers. Treat children as young people first, and deal with their specific gifts second.

3. Communication among the three groups of adults (parents, teachers, and counselors) is vital. Each group needs a clear understanding of the child and of the parents' and teacher's goals for the child. Different groups of adults often have different goals for the students. Consequently, it is important to share appropriate information with each other when making decisions.

4. Try to understand the social milieu of the school or classroom through the eyes of the child. This is difficult, but a worthwhile task. I have been astounded and dismayed by the extent to which the social expectations for students are never openly discussed or understood. Often, teachers and other school personnel have quite different views of what it means to be a student or a gifted student. Moreover, students also hold a wide variety of opinions about what they think being a student means, and how they should behave in various school settings. Therefore, talking openly about the social expectations for students can help them feel more comfortable in school.

5. Serve as a clearinghouse for information about gifted students and share the information and literature you've found via meetings. It is important to create opportunities for parents, teachers, and counselors to learn how to be proactive in the gifted child's life. The ERIC Clearinghouse has invaluable information prepared for this purpose. Other sources of information include local colleges and universities, state agencies, the National Association for Gifted Children, The Association for the Gifted, and the Internet.

6. Make individual, group, and family counseling available for gifted students and their families. Although it's relatively easy to organize such counseling, it is rarely done. You also can share materials with each group (parents, teachers, and counselors) as a means to better prepare the various professionals who work with gifted children.

7. Learn about the child's personality and social goals. This will enable all of you to guide the child throughout his or her school years. When pursuing this strategy, be sure to include information from the field of "general" psychology. The vast majority of facts within the field of psychology are often applicable to the lives of gifted students.

8. Teach the child to better understand his or her nature and anticipate how to react to events and circumstances in his or her life. Part of this understanding may be accomplished through personality and interest inventories. Astute adults in positions

to provide information based on observations of the child also may be able to help the child understand his or her nature.

9. Provide opportunities for gifted children to interact. This opportunity seems to alleviate some of the pressures a gifted child feels. For example, gifted students often report feeling different from other students, except when they spend time with other gifted students. They often comment on the profound sense of relief in knowing there are other people like themselves who have many similar interests and qualities.

I hope you find some of these ideas helpful as you work on behalf of gifted children. The next few chapters will continue this list of ideas to consider about the social and emotional needs of gifted students.

FOR DISCUSSION

- Consider the social expectations for a gifted preadolescent. In what way are they different from (or similar to) the social expectations of the gifted adolescent?

- Discuss the social milieu of the school or classroom with a gifted girl and a gifted boy. Are the social expectations different for girls and boys? How do their perspectives differ from your perspective of the social milieu of the school?

CHAPTER 11

Practical Advice for Guiding the Gifted

- Recognize and respect the relationship between social and emotional needs and academic needs.
- Be cautious about forcing your desires on students based on your perception of their strength areas.
- Teach social skills development.
- Teach gifted students to enjoy nonacademic activities.
- Teach gifted students ways to manage stress.
- Adults should model the behavior they wish gifted students to exhibit.
- Do not try to change the basic nature of the student.
- Embrace diversity, do not merely tolerate it.
- Expose gifted students to knowledgeable counseling.
- Know that coping strategies exist.
- Provide opportunities for down time.

The following was originally written as the second installment in a three-part series on the social and emotional needs of gifted students. Below are some ideas to consider as you attempt to guide the social and emotional development of gifted children.

1. Recognize and respect the relationship between students' social and emotional needs and academic needs. Each affects the other. For example, whether a gifted student is being challenged in class or able to work at a stimulating pace can affect

his or her emotional well-being. The school psychology clinic at the Teachers College at Ball State University has documented that the most common reason gifted students are referred for psychological assessments is because they have developed behavior problems in school after having previously been a strong student. The root of this change is their manifest frustration with not being challenged enough in school. For many students, this connection goes unnoticed until it is far too late to help them.

2. Be cautious about forcing your desires on students based on your perception of their strength areas. Talent manifests over time and with opportunity. Determining for a child what his or her "gift" or "talent" is without allowing for flexibility or encouraging additional self-exploration may cause a number of problems starting in adolescence. A positive outcome of nurturing a talent is the development of a lifelong interest or hobby.

3. Teaching gifted students a handful of social skills can reduce the number of negative experiences they may encounter while in school. Skills such as the phrasing of questions and comments and the ability to accept another person's perspective are skills that can help gifted students navigate the difficult social waters in schools.

4. Teach gifted children to enjoy nonacademic activities and to recognize that nonacademic pursuits are also important in life. Pursuits and hobbies can become stress relievers and additional areas where gifted students can grow.

5. Teach gifted students ways to manage stress. As they advance in grade levels, many will experience growing amounts of stress. Ironically, much of this will be self-imposed or a consequence of those around them only recognizing their gift without concern for their individuality. Because many gifted students develop coping strategies to deal with such stressors, educating them about how to effectively manage stress may prove relatively easy.

6. Adults should model the behaviors they wish gifted students to exhibit. Like all children, gifted students learn from the behavior of adults. Whether it is effective coping strategies, nonthreatening communication techniques, or just how to relax, teachers, counselors, and parents often become models that children can follow. If you want your messages to be influential, let the students see you behaving accordingly.

7. Understand that much of how gifted students appear and behave is biologically affected. Do not try to change the basic nature of the student. Shyness, for example, like some physical characteristics, has roots in biology. Like the relationship between body type and weight, shyness and a student's willingness and ability to actively participate in class are related.

8. Embrace diversity, do not merely tolerate it. To tolerate it suggests a position of authority or judgment that allows someone to decide what human differences are meaningful and acceptable, and what differences are intolerable. This special privileged position tends to disadvantage gifted students because giftedness rarely makes people's lists of meaningful differences. As a teacher, parent, or counselor, you are in a position to have a significant impact on the minds of gifted children. If a school truly embraces diversity, then gifted students will be accepted. In many schools, giftedness is still experienced as deviating from the norm. In a study a few years ago, I found that gifted students are just as prone to believe stereotypical ideas about other gifted students as the general population. This phenomenon can be explained by the fact that gifted students cannot escape their environment.

9. Expose gifted students to knowledgeable counseling, and avoid professionals who are not knowledgeable about gifted students. A proactive counseling program can be invaluable to gifted students. Learning about oneself and how to effectively relate to others in school can positively affect the psychological development of gifted students. Conversely, messages learned from counselors and psychologists untrained in gifted education

can actually exacerbate social and emotional problems for the gifted student.

10. Know that many gifted students will have created coping strategies while in the earliest grades in school. I have found that, by first grade, some gifted children have begun to engage in behavior patterns that reveal their discomfort with the gifted student label. Some of these strategies reflect their unspoken knowledge about the social milieu of their classroom. Knowing that these coping strategies exist can enable teachers, counselors, and parents to understand the worries and behaviors surrounding gifted students' school experience.

11. Provide opportunities for down time. All children need time to relax away from school concerns. Arranging down time for some students will come easily, but for others it will be quite difficult. Providing gifted students opportunities to explore their world or read for pleasure can reduce stress and may have the positive effect of increasing interest-based pursuits when they get older.

I hope you find some of these suggestions beneficial as you attempt to meet the social and emotional needs of gifted students. The next chapter will provide yet another list of considerations for parents, teachers, and counselors as they attempt the important task of meeting the psychological, social, and emotional needs of gifted students.

FOR DISCUSSION

- Reflect on some behaviors that you (as a parent, teacher, or counselor) model that are beneficial (or not so beneficial) for a gifted child or student.

- Ask the school psychologist or counselor what training he or she has in gifted education.

CHAPTER 12

Working on Behalf of Gifted Students

The following appeared as the third column in a series on meeting the social and emotional needs of gifted students. A number are somewhat specific to gifted students, while others might be just as effective with students of average ability. Some of the ideas respect biological influences while others emphasize environmental influences in this area. Clearly, only some of the ideas expressed across the three part series will be relevant for any specific student given his or her particular circumstances in life. Consequently, adults need to assess the relevance of these ideas to their students before attempting to pursue them.

1. Encourage controlled risk taking. Although it may seem to be an oxymoron, it really is not. Imagine the lives of professional stuntmen and women. These people earn a living by risking their lives, but do so with careful planning. They take obvious risks to their physical well-being, but they do so after great effort has gone into building safety nets and other precautions that minimize the potential for their harm. Similarly, gifted students need to take risks to build same- and opposite-sex

friendships and to communicate with other students and teachers. To engage in this type of social risk taking, safeguards need to be in place. Parents, teachers, and counselors can help create those "safety nets." For example, building an environment of acceptance in a classroom and school establishes a climate that supports emotional and social risk taking. This suggestion dovetails into the next one.

2. Provide a variety of social experiences for gifted students. Together, adults can orchestrate situations where gifted students interact with a wide variety of people. These types of experiences will build social skills needed in specific contexts and help develop the gifted students' social cognition. As the students have positive experiences, their self-concepts also will be enhanced.

3. Inventory family similarities and differences as compared to schoolmates. In some school settings, the diversity is obvious, while in others it is not. It can be helpful to gifted students to know what their family's values, practices, and beliefs are and how these vary from those of other groups of people. If discussed within the context of diversity, then their giftedness can be accepted as quite normal, rather than aberrant.

4. To accomplish the previous suggestion, one approach is to encourage gifted students to read biographies of eminent people. This is considered a form of bibliotherapy. The details provided in the biographies will often cause two events to occur. The consciousness of the gifted student will be raised concerning the experiences that impacted the eminent person's development. For example, some of the scientists in Germany prior to World War II speak about their lives as Jews during the rise of Hitler and the strong anti-Semitism that pervaded Germany. Reading biographies allows students to compare their lives with that of the person in the biography, and raises awareness that many highly accomplished people also struggled with some of the same issues the students face. This realization tends to reduce feelings of isolation while at the same time providing ideas for dealing with the difficulties gifted people

encounter. Part of the potential effectiveness of this approach is that the reader becomes actively engaged in the story and creates his or her own understanding of the issues he or she faces. This is a vastly different experience from having one's parent discuss issues with you. Although both reading biographies and discussing issues of diversity with parents can be successful, using both approaches may prove more beneficial than relying on only one.

5. A second approach for educating gifted students about diversity is to provide mentorship opportunities. Apprenticeships can have many positive effects, including the building of numerous skills. In this example, it is important to note the students' connection with the mentor's life story. Working with a mentor teaches many lessons, including who the mentor is as an individual and what pathway he or she followed to establish this identity, from the mentor's own perspective. Through this person's life story, issues in the individual development of the mentor can be recognized and understood by the gifted student. Like the effects of bibliotherapy, connecting with a significant adult who represents an academic area of interest to a gifted student offers many opportunities for the student to appreciate and navigate the social and emotional waters of his or her life.

6. Love and respect gifted students for who they are. Then, emphasize the idea of doing rather than being; ability and talent are neutral constructs, while doing is virtuous. Try to help them understand that being academically able does not make a person good or bad, per se. Rather, like many characteristics, it is *how* people strive to develop and subsequently use other abilities that make them virtuous. It is important for both gifted students and others to develop their talents in and outside of academics. An overemphasis by the three groups of adults (teachers, parents, and counselors) on the students' abilities tends to create feelings by gifted students that they are nothing *but* their academic ability or achievement. This can lead to many problems, including underachievement, unnec-

essary suffering when doing poorly in school, the unwillingness to stretch beyond areas of prior attainment, and identity foreclosure. Identity foreclosure is the result of deciding at too young an age where to emphasize one's professional aspirations. Deciding to pursue math as a career because early in life a student is taught that he or she is particularly able in that area will often lead to the student choosing not to risk failure in other areas. Hence, other potential talent areas are never identified. Negative patterns within careers also exist for many people who decided on their career path too early in life.

7. Encourage a self-concept that extends far beyond the academic self-concept. It is never beneficial to convince a gifted student that only his or her academic achievement is valuable. What good to society is a person who can calculate advanced math problems at an early age, but who has developed no civic responsibilities? Although I do not accept the claim that schools should attempt to equally develop the "whole" person, I do believe that gifted students should be appreciated as children who develop over time and, consequently, deserve the right to develop various aspects of their being. As in every preceding example, parents, teachers and counselors need to work together for this suggestion to be realized.

Teachers, parents, and counselors should recognize the important roles they play in the psychological development of gifted students. Gifted students will develop with or without adult guidance. The question is "How will they develop without coordinated guidance that is underpinned by research in developmental psychology and informed research on gifted students' lives in school?" My answer is that it is inconceivable that they can develop effectively and painlessly without the support of their parents, teachers, and counselors. Let us commit to supporting the psychological development of all students, including gifted students.

FOR DISCUSSION

- As a parent, teacher, or counselor, consider whether you provide opportunities for social risk taking for gifted individuals.

- Compile a list of three (or more) biographies of gifted individuals that you have read or would like to read. Share them with other teachers or parents in order to compile an extensive list to use with your student or child.

CHAPTER 13

Developing Relationships, Communication, and Identity

KEY CONCEPTS

- Improving communication through journaling and artistic expression
- Building relationships
- Developing identity

For this chapter, I have divided the suggestions that teachers, parents, and counselors can consider as they work on behalf of gifted students into four groups: (1) improving communication, (2) building relationships, (3) developing identity, and (4) suggestions for adults. Many of the ideas are equally applicable to gifted students and students of average ability.

Improving Communication

One of the most effective approaches to improving the communication between gifted students and adults, and between gifted students and other students, is to encourage the expression of thoughts and feelings.

For many years, journaling has been used to elicit ideas and the exchange of thoughts and feelings between a teacher and student. Therapists have also used journals to gain insight into their clients' lives and to assist their clients in the self-reflection process.

The communication between both groups (student/adult, student/other students) can be improved through journaling when the adult establishes goals for a student's journal and encourages student participation.

A simple note of warning is called for here. Attempting to improve communication by reading a student's private journal (diary) will hurt, rather than improve, communication. The student is likely to feel violated by the adult, and he or she will most likely minimize communication for some period of time afterward.

Another way to improve communication is to create opportunities for the student to express him- or herself through artistic means. Again, this approach has a long, rich history in the field of psychology as a means of reaching difficult clients and in helping clients heal. I strongly encourage adults to use these techniques as stimuli only and not as diagnostic tools. The immediate benefit will be derived from the conversations enabled by the process and products, not from any diagnosis made by the adult.

Building Relationships

Gifted students often feel that they have few friends with similar interests. Technological breakthroughs, particularly e-mail, have made communicating with others around the globe both immediate and inexpensive. I encourage adults to look for ways to assist in the interactions of gifted students with others via e-mail.

This process is becoming increasingly common as teachers have their students create electronic pen pals as part of class assignments. These relationships are typically well-managed and quite safe for the students. Friendly relationships emerge as a natural consequence of gifted students meeting others like themselves. Tales abound of the friendships created during specialized programs such as Governor's Schools or other summer residential programs that are sustained by using e-mail.

The more traditional approach of encouraging pen pal relationships by postal service still provides options for gifted students to build relationships with others who have similar interests. The traditional mail approach adds an additional level of safety, although it sacrifices the immediacy of using electronic mail. Both can work, but both need adult supervision.

In addition to developing relationships with other people, many benefits can be derived from giving students a pet. The relationship that often develops between children and pets is known to be very important in students' development of personal responsibility, compassion, and empathy. Students also can benefit from the basic companionship having a pet provides.

Developing Identity

There are numerous ways of assisting in the development of a student's identity. Some are relatively easy to bring about, while others are much more difficult. Many adults may be unaware that gifted children often become concerned with ethical considerations of life at an earlier age than is common for most children. Adults often are surprised by the child's concerns, and sometimes they will make light of them. Anticipating and dealing honestly and empathetically with young children who are struggling with these worries can be very important to their development.

Gifted students should be encouraged to have an active life outside of school. There are benefits to both outside activities that remain separate from school and those that have some connection to school. For example, learning to play musical instruments can originate in or out of school, and the potential transfer back and forth is generally a positive experience in building identity. Other parallel experiences include sports-related activities, such as soccer, baseball, football, and so forth. Sports, for those interested, can help develop a positive sense of identity. I do, however, stress the need for the child to be interested in playing the sport. Lack of interest, even when a student has ability, does not nurture skill development. This leaves a student vulnerable to embarrassment. Few experiences are more difficult for children than to fail repeatedly in front of friends, family, and other people.

A third suggestion is to respect children's passions, especially as they grow older. With young children, parents effectively control the children's activities. Consequently, the children tend to have options for activities that are of some interest to their families.

As students get older, they are allowed to explore more, potentially developing interests outside of their parents' desires. Balancing the time and energy needed to develop any area of endeavor is difficult. Parents need to allow the time for interests to develop, even when they are not the parents' interests. Respecting the passions of gifted students will assist in the development of their self-concepts and feelings of self-efficacy and agency.

A very important quality for healthy adults is empathy. Some gifted children have an abundance of empathy, while others need to be taught. Teaching empathy is not easy, but it can be done.

As noted in a previous chapter, helping students develop a sophisticated understanding of human diversity can reduce the pain and suffering of gifted children as they realize that being different is both the norm and the exception; it is the norm in the infinite ways people differ, and the exception when one is seeking people who have similar interests, qualities, or beliefs.

Empathy for the lives of others enables gifted children to more fully appreciate that people have psychological needs that are similar to their own. Without empathy, gifted children can come to believe that they are completely estranged from others because the more obvious differences (e.g., academic passions) will dominate their perspectives of others.

One approach to developing empathy is to engage the child in an activity where each person assumes the perspective of another. Over time, the conditions can be changed so that difficult situations can be experienced vicariously to the extent necessary to build empathy.

For the Adults

I include the following suggestions because an unintended implication is that, if you follow the ideas outlined in this chapter, the gifted child will not suffer. As a psychologist, researcher, and parent, the hardest lesson I have had to learn is the inevitability of pain and suffering experienced by some gifted children. This realization can elicit feelings of inadequacy and impotence in the adults around them.

I encourage the three groups of adults (parents, teachers, and counselors) to work diligently to assist in the development of gifted children, but to be prepared for the difficulties of life. Constant communication can have a positive impact because many of life's difficulties will emerge from the child interacting in the adults' environments. Modeling calmness and caring may prove to be the best practice when students are suffering with the normal trials and tribulations of life.

By being aware of the social and emotional needs of our young people, we will be better able to effectively guide their development. Let us continue to attempt to help all children enjoy rich and full lives, including gifted children.

FOR DISCUSSION

- Reflect on whether you provide opportunities for gifted children/students to express themselves artistically. Do you encourage them to participate in activities that are unrelated to their "talent" or "gift"?

CHAPTER 14

Swagger or Humility or Swagger and Humility: A New Goal for Educating Students With Gifts and Talents

KEY CONCEPTS

- The result of asking intellectually talented students to develop and manifest swagger may be humility

- Gifted students should test their mettle with other great students

- The benefits of gifted students working as a team

THE YEAR WAS 2081, and everybody was finally equal. They weren't only equal before God and the law. They were equal every which way. Nobody was smarter than anybody else. Nobody was better looking than anybody else. Nobody was stronger or quicker than anybody else. All this equality was due to the 211th, 212th, and 213th Amendments to the Constitution, and to the unceasing vigilance of agents of the United States Handicapper General. (Vonnegut, 1961)

Vonnegut's story *Harrison Bergeron* is a clever way of satirizing society's naïve notion of egalitarianism and the effects it has on the development of children. As an aging professor who focuses on the psychology of gifted students, I have observed many gifted students in many different environments. A year ago I watched a team of outstanding eighth-grade volleyball players, including several academically gifted students, perform its magic on the court. Once again, they easily beat their opponent, but more importantly, it was their behavior and dispositions that I found noteworthy. This was a group of twelve 13-year-old girls who emanated confidence. To describe them as a mere team does not do them justice. They were a gang. Their relationships with each other had rules and expectations. They were great as individual players; but they were even greater as a team. They walked around with their heads way up, backs arched—almost strutting. They were manifesting—dare I say, swagger. A person manifesting swagger exudes pride and confidence. It is an audacious manner and you see it in the highly accomplished from all occupations.

To understand why the girls' swagger matters, it must be put into its context. These young athletes play volleyball for the Burris Laboratory School (Burris), a part of Teachers College at Ball State University. Burris is a K–12 school with 500 students. The high school volleyball team has won 18 state championships, including 10 in a row. Moreover, they have won four national championships and were runners-up on three occasions. The coach of the high school team has a record of approximately 1,070 and 88, including the 2004 national champions, who went 40 and 0. Years ago, a community volleyball program was started that attempted to develop the talent of hundreds of young girls. Over the past 20 years, the success has spread to several other programs surrounding Muncie, IN (a small city of about 65,000 inhabitants), with several state championships being won across the different classes of schools. Making the Burris high school volleyball team accomplishments even more impressive is the fact that students cannot transfer into the school. Students are admitted through a lottery system as kindergartners, and then some siblings can get in when there are openings. This means that Burris cannot recruit any student athletes; they coach the players they have.

The team of eighth-grade girls exists therefore as athletes roughly at the midpoint of this talent development model. Perhaps it is more accurate to describe it as a talent development community. Consequently, their swagger is in the context of being outstanding, dedicated athletes within a community of extraordinary support of girls' athletic talent. By this point in their lives, they have played volleyball for several years. Unlike the citizens of Harrison Bergeron's society, their talents have been lauded and nurtured. They have been allowed to excel and rewarded with attention and respect. Do intellectually gifted children have similar opportunities?

Juxtaposition With Academic Talent Development

It is believed by many that unsophisticated notions of elitism are the bane of the field of gifted education. Some claims of elitism are based on an interpretation of the founding of our country as inherently egalitarian. Educational opportunities that are tailored to student abilities are determined to be inherently elitist and therefore antiegalitarian. Humility often is described as a corollary to egalitarianism. Obviously then, swagger would not be acceptable to those who hold these beliefs. This concern only seems to hold in the context of schooling, especially as it pertains to gifted students. For example, we reward professional athletes in some sports who become infamous due to their outrageous behavior (e.g., steroid use). The better they become known, the more we expect them to violate decorum and the more we reward them for doing so. This has been true for so long now that social expectations have actually changed to accommodate the extremes. In the early stages of the development of these professional athletes, swagger was evident but kept under wraps. Once athletics move from the so-called amateur ranks to the professional, a shift in the expectations of both the athlete and the audience occurs. Some professional athletes, while revered by their audience for their extraordinary abilities, are actually rewarded when they act in some socially inappropriate ways.

A commonality in the development of great athletes and great intellects is the fact that much of their training and opportunities to develop occur within our school communities. They sit side by side and sometimes quite literally in the same seat (student-athletes) in the classroom. Some athletes are so talented that they develop quickly and are embraced by professionals right out of high school (e.g., LeBron James), but most continue their development into their college years—again, along with those developing their great minds. The incubator of talent creates differing scripts for appropriate behavior across the varying domains of talent, but with more in common than different. As the talented emerge into their respective professional ranks, they are reborn into a world of vastly different cultures. Although many cultures of work exist, each with rules and regulations, swagger is manifest and even expected in many that celebrate world-class achievement. For example, we expect our athletes to exude confidence. They even engage in pregame rituals to raise their adrenalin to enhance their focus, confidence, and readiness for performance. *They are cultivating swagger to help elevate performance.*

What if we inserted the expectation into our models of developing the talent of our intellectually gifted students that they must develop and manifest swagger? To do so would mean the internalization of pride, the value of hard work, an awareness of their own strengths and weaknesses, an appreciation of the role of struggle in achievement, an incremental notion of giftedness, compassion, an appreciation of others' abilities, and, yes, humility. To understand greatness, one must be able to recognize it in others. Being appreciative of the greatness of others does not diminish the growth of the aspirant; it creates humility and it becomes a step in the direction of developing the talents of the individual. Requiring our intellectually gifted youth to maintain humility without swagger dooms them to ignorance as it inserts an unnecessary and disingenuous impediment to world-class performance. Not being able to recognize brilliance does not create egalitarianism, it creates mediocre performance. I have learned that it is an essential ingredient for intellectually gifted students to test their mettle with other great students. Requiring them to take stock in, and not to feign ignorance of, their own capabilities, both as an individual and as part of a team, will help in the development of their talents. To become world-class one must be able to recognize it. Humility should be rooted in being informed, not in ignorance. Therefore, humility and swagger are merely two sides of the same coin.

Of course, I am not advocating that we teach our children to become arrogant, hostile, or misbehaving. Manners and grace are laudable qualities. I am merely encouraging us to become more sophisticated about talent development and to not focus on the unimportant behaviors that intuitively may seem undesirable. When Don Imus made his ridiculous remarks in 2007 about the Rutgers women's basketball team, I knew from observing the eighth-grade versions of those fine athletes that they were going to do just fine. Don Imus was no match for the swagger (confidence, pride, poise, and resiliency) and humility (based on understanding the necessity of hard work and struggle on the path to becoming highly accomplished) that come from developing talents both as individuals and as a team.

FOR DISCUSSION

- What would need to change in our schools in order for intellectually gifted students to exhibit pride, to be able to swagger?

- Are there ways in which students with gifts and talents benefit from staying "under the radar"?

- Athletics is often heralded by educators of the gifted as offering the model of talent development to emulate. Discuss the pros and cons of such a model.

CHAPTER 15

Putting the Well-Being of All Students (Including Gifted Students) First

- The meaning of *well-being*
- Well-being for gifted children in the school context
- Learning at appropriate rates and in appropriate environments

What if we put the well-being of individual students (including gifted students) first in planning and carrying out school activities? How would things be different? These two questions seem innocuous at first, but upon further inspection, the answers may, in fact, require radical departures from current thinking and practice.

Preface

In my judgment, one of the most existential events that occurs in life is learning. *Existentialism* is defined as a "philosophical theory emphasizing the existence of the individual person as a free and responsible agent determining his or her own development" (Allen, 1996, p. 506). We do it by ourselves. An individual must change in order to learn. Others can either facilitate or impede an individual's learning, but only the individual can literally make it happen. In essence, learning is a personal experience that professional educators should try to facilitate by using the best educational practices known. Sometimes this requires us to reconsider and question our beliefs and practices. One such question to ask ourselves is "What if we put the well-being of the individual student (including gifted students) first in planning and carrying out school activities?"

Let us begin by noting the arguments many have raised against the idea of schools putting the well-being of individuals first:

◈ we cannot organize schools around the needs of every student individually;

◈ this would be too expensive, too difficult, too cumbersome, and too complicated;

◈ it would cause too many scheduling problems;

◈ it would hurt sports or band; and

◈ why have it as a goal anyway because (gifted) students need to learn how to adapt to the real world, rather than expecting the world to adapt to their needs?

I lump these concerns under the heading of "ideas that require school leaders to move beyond their comfort zone" and, therefore, these ideas generally fail.

Context

So, what if schools decided to focus on the well-being of their gifted students as individuals first? Before they could do that, a few questions would need to be answered. For example, what exactly does well-being mean? Most schools already claim to look after the well-being of all of their students; they just do not ascribe to the goal of individual needs driving decision making and determining practice. In essence, we leave decisions on defining well-being to local school boards and state departments of education. This then gets handed off to achievement on the growing number of states' minimum-competency tests. Hence, *well-being* often is defined as reaching minimum competency on a statewide achievement test, a definition that rarely has positive effects in the lives of gifted students. Local school districts then decide how to spend their budget to assist their students in reaching minimum competency. As the old saying goes, "We measure what we treasure."

Question: How many states' minimum-competency testing initiatives were originated by teachers? Answer: None. Typically, state legislatures create bills to this end. These efforts are usually supported, if not pushed, by state chambers of commerce. Hence, a competing notion of well-being from the state's financial communities is often that our students are part of the equation that should provide business owners a competitive edge. Consequently, children are educated at the same time that two very different notions of what is in their best interest are being held. It would be nice to think that battles are raging over these competing ideas, but unfortunately the commerce-based notion of well-being has ended the argument with the advent of minimum-competency testing.

It was recently reported in an Indiana newspaper that state legislators were seeking a law that would criminalize any behavior under the heading of improper testing practices—including teaching to the test—relative to the state's achievement test. If this occurs, teachers whose livelihood is already contingent upon the scores of their students on this minimum-competency test could go to jail if they teach to the test. How does this position stack up with another significant national educational movement, often sponsored by those who wish to determine school outcomes—the College Board? More specifically, the College Board-sponsored Advanced Placement (AP) courses, the courses' respective tests, and the faculty members who teach the courses could not be more closely interconnected. AP faculty regularly use practice tests made up of items from previous exams and are encouraged to do so. In addition, they are asked to grade vast numbers of the same tests their own students take. So, why is teaching to the test at the minimum competency level so scandalous, and at the most advanced level of instruction, desirable? Teachers are "damned if they do, and damned if they don't." I guess the key is timing. Ironically, neither of these approaches puts the individual student's needs first.

De Facto Goals of Schools

As is always the case, we have intrepid teachers who want what is best for their students. They move within the cultures of their schools, districts, and state rules and regulations, and under the umbrella of their states' minimum-competency testing expectations. Although there is clear evidence that many teachers are willing to experiment with their classroom organization and pedagogy on behalf of their students, it has historically been a problem that some of the recommended practices on behalf of gifted students exceed the individual teacher's ability. For example, grade skipping (single and multiple) and course skipping depend upon support from other teachers and administrators. They also depend upon the wishes of parents—an important consideration when weighing these two options. Teachers have responded to these and other concerns by literally and metaphorically shutting their classroom doors. This is a reaction to external limitations and a desire to control their own classroom environment, an environment subject to the preferences of a number of political and education-based groups. Although sometimes a necessity, this reaction often leaves few options and little support for gifted students to have an individualized education.

Making matters even more difficult for teachers are the expectations we have of them. James Gallagher once told me that teachers of gifted children are expected to be experts in all manifestations of how children vary and are expected to be able to teach them just as effectively across all setting variables. In other words, our students must rely on the standard that every single teacher of the gifted must be extraordinary for the system to work.

Classroom Options

What is left for gifted students in this closed-door environment? Individual teacher attention, a differentiated curriculum, and cluster grouping are a few options available to the teacher. Outside enrichment options, such as Saturday and summer special programs, afterschool clubs and activities, and mentorships, also may remain. In short, teachers have only some control over whether a school will try to meet the needs of individual students, gifted included.

Social and Emotional Lessons Learned

The model of teaching to minimum competency has inherent limitations on gifted students. For example, as the school day progresses, boredom ensues and lessons are implied, such as that being passionate about learning is not valued in school—in fact, it may be counterproductive. Knowledge of the most rudimentary facts and processes are believed to be more valued and welcome in the classroom than advanced knowledge or skills.

How long does it take gifted students to realize that they are going to be taught (long before any effort will be made to find out) what they already know and are able to do? We turn a collective blind eye to the messages that we send gifted students.

In essence, being passionate about academics holds no currency in schools that plan for the masses and put their focus on minimum-competency tests. What does hold value in such a setting? Compliance, complacency, a friendly outgoing personality, and enthusiasm for work ing in groups are valued. Showing interest and participating in "in-the-moment," teacher-led activities, plus "going along," are often the messages learned.

Add to these in-school perceptions the mixed messages that gifted students often perceive, such as "all kids are gifted," "no kids are gifted," "gifted kids have unfair advantages," and "gifted kids can get it on their own," and you have an idea of a gifted child's perceptions of school—*child* being the operative word here. Children learn these lessons even when they are unintended. In schools that do not plan for the nature, needs, and knowledge of the individual child, underachievement is prevalent, as is a growing sense of self-doubt and students feeling undervalued.

Examining Common Terms

Acceleration

With all this in context, what does the commonly used term *acceleration* mean? From the individual child's perspective, it does not mean anything. What if we changed the term acceleration to the phrase *opportunity to learn at appropriate rates*? It is easy to see the change that perspective makes here. In other words, from the child's perspective, he or she would really experience school as appropriately challenging, but would remain confident when working on the material at hand. This experience is quite the opposite of what is described above and would yield considerable social and emotional benefits to all students, especially gifted students.

Should parents and teachers avoid grade skipping or course skipping out of their worries that a student is not socially or emotionally ready and such measures would be damaging to the child? Although adults should be concerned about the well-being of their children, this worry is most often just a projection of the adults, and does not have a high likelihood of occurring. In other words, on what basis is this worry substantiated? At any age and in every classroom, there is a wide variation of children's social and emotional development. We have all known young children who are socially or emotionally mature or older children who are immature in these areas. Teachers see these variations in their classes daily. Research indicates that only in rare instances are gifted children negatively affected socially or emotionally when they are accelerated. With proper training, teachers should be able to deal effectively with social and emotional variations among their students. Consequently, a student who is able to master the course content more quickly than others should not present a problem when grouped with older students, some of whom may be on the same social or emotional level.

School Mission and Teaching and Administrative Practice

Clearly, people are social beings and schools are learning environments; therefore, schools are social learning environments. Public schools also are institutions supported by tax dollars. Are they intended to be optimal learning environments, the best learning environments that can be had on shoestring budgets, or institutions to prepare less-fortunate children for working-class jobs? Are they led by academic ideals, or for social acculturation goals? Teaching and administrative practices often reveal those intentions actually being pursued.

Cooperative Learning

If students have the opportunity to learn at appropriate rates, then what does this say about the practice of cooperative learning? Should students be accelerated to work with students at their same ability level, or should they be grouped with students of lesser ability to work on projects?

Our practices and strategies are based on certain assumptions. Some are tacit assumptions, while others are more commonly known. For example, are cooperative-learning techniques employed as a means to assist in the optimal academic development of each student? I would argue that they are not. They represent grouping techniques used for broad social reasons (e.g., gifted students need to learn how to work with less able others, or they will master the subject better by teaching it to their peers, a belief that many teachers hold). Cooperative learning also is used with goals of enriching the curriculum. From the student's perspective, however, cooperative learning often teaches gifted students the following lessons:

✦ I am expected to do the work of the teacher,

✦ the lesson is going to be at a low level, and

✦ extra knowledge and skills are not appreciated in this classroom.

Gifted students often experience being the workhorse for the less serious and capable students in the cooperative-learning groups—they have to carry the group. Does this really happen in schools? As a parent of gifted children, I can report that I have witnessed this as the pattern in classrooms, rather than the exception, and I have had to counsel my children when they felt great duress after carrying their learning groups.

Acceleration and cooperative learning would mean different things to students if the practices and beliefs surrounding these concepts emerged from the needs of the individual child rather than from many other influences. Challenging gifted students in highly systematic and informed ways, wherein learning takes place just within the intellectual reach of the child, should be our schools' approach. Pretesting before instruction and making decisions about classroom practices and school organization based on the well-being of individual students will improve the quality of learning for all students. This would help to bring out the best in every child (including gifted children), and it would reduce underachievement issues, such as lowered self-concept and feelings of being undervalued.

FOR DISCUSSION

- As a teacher, counselor, or parent, reflect on and discuss how well-being is defined in the school environment. Who defines it?

- Discuss what is done in the school to foster the well-being of gifted children.

CHAPTER 16

Owning the Problem of Undesirable Behavior: Disintermediation and How Our Children Are Taught to Drink, Smoke, and Gamble

KEY CONCEPTS

- Developing new social norms
- The role of behaviorism and adult models
- Helping gifted kids develop positive values

Recently I was thinking about how our society is teaching our children to gamble. Although I hold no strong personal views about gambling per se, it struck me that our school-age children are growing up within a culture where most voices expressed on the matter indicate a value that they would rather risk money with a very low possibility of return than pay taxes. Although a false dichotomy, the values expressed often become clarified at the level of school support. That is, our states' populations would rather gamble with a slight chance of winning something and a larger possibility of losing than pay taxes to support schools through more secure, conventional property tax models. My consciousness about this matter was raised with the argument made by the self-proclaimed arbiter of virtues, William Bennett, who disclosed that he had lost well more than a million dollars gambling. This column is not about virtues or taxes, but an analysis of how and what we are teaching our children, intentionally or otherwise.

Children learn societal norms and values through observing the behaviors of more knowledgeable peers and adults and through both operant and classical conditioning. The many years of psychology dedicated to behaviorism has taught us that behaviors are shaped by repeated pairing of a stimulus with a response (classical conditioning) and by rewarding or punishing behaviors (operant conditioning). Despite our knowledge of the effect of our own behavior, there is evidence in the popular culture that many adults are neglecting their role in shaping the attitudes and behaviors of their children through modeling and conditioning. When adults sanction gambling as a legitimate activity for funding schools, children are watching and learning.

I will continue by offering a long list of life lessons we teach our children that translate into attitudes and behaviors. Although some of these examples are axiomatic, the accumulation of the lessons learned needs our serious consideration. Through adult examples, in addition to teaching our children to value and engage in gambling, we have done the same for smoking, drinking, sex, steroids, growth hormones, cheating in school, and so forth. These behaviors are controlled exclusively by adults, and adults must take responsibility for the effects that our behavior has on children. It is fair to conclude that our children's attitudes are shaped by the adults who raise them, the culture they are growing up within that includes the various forms of media they are exposed to, and the students' referent groups.

Like most industries, the culture our children are being raised in is controlled by adults with agendas. Making money most often is a primary goal. For example, when children are taught to smoke, drink, or gamble by those who market such enterprises, making money is the goal. Some might argue that it is not the direct intention to teach children to engage in the same behaviors that adults are being drawn into. I find this to be a disingenuous position similar to the argument that declaring a war does not create the conditions that elicit rape, pillage, and multiple forms of atrocities such as torture. In both examples, history is clear that one leads to the other. Therefore, with state-run gambling and the multitude of activities and platitudes surrounding it, no one should be surprised that the rates of gambling addiction in children are on the increase. The modeling alone signifies to children what is valued in society.

The profit goal sheds light on the overall lesson being learned: The use of money for individual interests, passions, and even addictions is better for society than working with a communitarian mentality. As Gore Vidal once said in an interview, describing his take on America of the late 1900s, "First one acquires wealth, then he acquires virtue."

What does our society teach our children and how does it occur? I mentioned gambling, smoking, drinking, sex, steroids, and growth hormones. I will add to the list some more lessons that I have discerned from watching television, reading papers and magazines, and observing and interviewing students: It is better to be infamous as a buffoon than to exist less famously as a competent professional; long-term relationships are not important; collaboration only is to be encouraged when all else fails; being a serious student is for social outcasts; cheating as a means to an end is acceptable; appearance/image is everything; taking advantage of any person one can is justified and even expected; and the individual is all that matters. In essence, a type of nihilism that conflates freedom, individualism, and wealth has become commonplace.

A pernicious example of adults teaching dubious behaviors to children is the unbridled marketing of "energy drinks" to minors. I was in a setting recently where young musicians were honing their skills and performing in an alcohol-free location. A highly decorated Austin Mini Cooper pulled up to the venue. Two young, attractive females emerged and began plying the children with free cans of Red Bull. This is an example of the basic approach taken by those who market to our children. In essence, they are trying to create a desire where one did not exist before. In this example, a product that gets considerable airplay on television is introduced in a setting that has added social desirability (being associated with successful rock musicians), with an element of risk or mimicking adult behavior, but in a young person's reference. In this form of marketing, the primary goal is disintermediation, the elimination of anything that might exist between the marketer and the person being marketed to (i.e., parents). In psychological terms, the process used to elicit the desired behavior is representative of operant conditioning. Marketers of energy drinks model their practice on this kind of conditioning. The subject is introduced to the product in a setting that is to be associated with the product (in this case a musical setting populated mostly by children and adolescents). The specific brand is given away so the children will experience the drink during an event that is somewhat emotionally charged. Each person is allowed/encouraged to take some additional cans to "share with friends." A perfect association is made. The drink is positively associated with the locale, music, and musicians—their most powerful referent group (others with similar passions and of a similar age)—and, because the drink generally is discouraged verbally by adults due to its stated purpose of heightened energy, and for the chemicals that make it up, the drink carries an element of added excitement for the young people when they drink it. Producers also wish to market the drink as new and part of the youth culture.

I tested the effectiveness of the marketing model by offering to provide some of the children I had accompanied with bottles of water or soft drinks, and not one chose that option. They preferred to drink the energy drink (be initiated to this beverage and be a part of an event where virtually everyone else was drinking same beverage at the same time), even though they grimaced with each swallow. It was clear that some found the drink to be quite distasteful. This example represents the power of social influences on youth. Being accepted and feeling a part of a desired group leads children (and adults) to engage in all sorts of questionable behavior.

The marketing approach for energy drinks is similar to that used to teach children to smoke. The initial experiences that most young people have with their first few cigarettes is that of distaste in the mouth and throat and harshness on the lungs. Given this, why do they continue to the point of an addiction? Marketers have known the answer to this question for decades: The power of the referent group and social influences affect a person's behavior. Cigarettes, like gambling and more recently energy drinks, must be associated with desired outcomes long enough for the habit to develop and, later, for addiction to occur.

Adolescents tend to value authenticity and individualism over most other matters. Teaching members of my generation to smoke was easy given the ways in which movies and television provided constant role models. Psychological associations of smoking and sex and smoking and strength were so common that the pairings have been cliché for decades. This health risk is one that has been addressed fairly aggressively, but there remain models and encouragement for many young people to take up the habit. The potency of the modeling is made much stronger when members of a referent group (e.g., their rebellious peers) smoke.

Drinking may be the most accepted adult behavior that children engage in. With my experience in higher education over the past 25 years, it is clear to me that college students talk about drinking (mostly in terms of binges) in many of their conversations. Campuses with no tolerance for alcohol find ways to ignore its widespread use and tolerate drinking in fraternities. I have seen administrators actually smuggle alcohol into university functions against the policies of the university. Although I do not hold strong moralistic views about drinking, it is the hypocrisy and the mixed messages that our children are exposed to that have reinforced their drinking behavior. Our lukewarm and often contradictory positions, ranging from a hellfire and brimstone approach to a wink and a nod, contribute to reinforcing this behavior. We have taught them to value drinking alcohol.

What are the lessons to be learned for rearing students with gifts and talents? For decades, psychologists have demonstrated the development of our young children through young adulthood as having several predictable qualities. Developing an identity is critical in the psychosocial development of the person. Knowing that can serve as a useful tool in predicting choices that will be made based on the models available. Consequently, modeling is very important in affecting our growing children's sense of self.

Teaching students with gifts and talents to develop wisdom about themselves and the world should be our goal. My advice at this time is to ask the three groups of adults (teachers, counselors, and parents) to first become more conscious of the large-scale influences that encourage the behaviors that I have catalogued. Second, I would ask that the adults take stock in their personal values regarding these matters, as well as other important topics. Once clear, I suggest that they engage youth in thoughtful dialogue about these matters. During these discussions, the adults will need to prepare themselves for the points that naturally will be made (i.e., that our children are merely doing what we do, but in a more modern way, such as drinking energy drinks in lieu of coffee). I suggest that when adults have concerns about the values being taught by marketers, or about any other aspect of our society, the issues should be discussed until positions are clearly understood. This can be accomplished in the process of teaching students how to recognize both efforts at marketing to them and the power of social environments. The adults will need to model the desired outcomes themselves to provide the consistency necessary to both stimulate and reinforce behavior in the children. In essence, I am asking for a type of ongoing engagement that is labor intensive and that may cut across the adult's personal behavior. Stated more directly, I am asking that we become good role models for the behaviors that we believe to be important and that we become increasingly more sophisticated about societal influences on everyone.

Our children are growing up at a time in history when there is absolutely unbridled marketing for their attention. Whether through traditional ads on television or more contemporary ads on telephones or computer screens, marketing aimed at affecting our children's behavior is everywhere. Offering models of successful adults that represent our values may prove to be the way to successfully raise all students, including those with gifts and talents.

FOR DISCUSSION

- Are gifted adolescents in some way protected from or immune to the outside forces influencing positive or negative behaviors and attitudes?

- What do you think the role of adults should be in helping to shape the values of gifted children and adolescents?

CHAPTER 17

Self-Mutilation and Gifted Children

KEY CONCEPTS

- Self-mutilation as an indication of emotional distress
- Differences between self-mutilation and self-expression

About 20 years ago, I came to believe that, while there are many similarities in the development of current students and that of previous generations, there are significant differences in the experiences of every generation of students. More primal than cohort-based experiences of any group are the lived experiences of the individual. Adding to this recipe of difference are the historical ingredients that change over time. Lived experiences will differ greatly among people growing up in different times. For example, growing up in a time of war or peace makes a difference in lived experience. Growing up when advanced technology is manifest in a four-function calculator or current-day laptop computers makes a difference in lived experience. Growing up when cultural appearance and social mores are transmitted primarily in one's home or throughout the media makes a difference in lived experience. Growing up when communication among youth is primarily between two friends in close proximity by telephone, or among two people of varying ages who communicate through the computer from locations in different states or even different countries, makes a difference in lived experience. Growing up when Americans believed that torture was wholly unacceptable, and a time when the value and support for the use of torture is actually touted by a sizeable number of Americans, makes a difference in lived experience.

115

Consequently, when one attempts to understand behavior, it must be considered in context. An example of contemporary behaviors that are relatively different than those of previous generations is the growth in frequency of many forms of self-mutilation. Some examples include cutting, scratching, picking at scabs or cuts, ingesting toxic materials, and pinching that causes bruising. The term *mutilation* sometimes reflects the intergenerational bias that comes from values perspectives that differ by generation. In other words, the term self-mutilation is sometimes perceived as quite offensive by the younger cohort group. Many who conduct research or provide theory in this area prefer the term *self-injury*. Some forms of these behaviors, such as cutting or scratching, could be described as physical self-mutilation. Other contemporary behaviors such as branding, piercing, and body sculpting (strategically placing metal pins just below the skin to create images) can be well described by two terms: self-mutilation and self-expression. In this column I will introduce these topics, giving attention to the behaviors generally held to be more hurtful than expressive—cutting and scratching. I first became aware of these behaviors through firsthand experience. As the executive director of a public residential academy for intellectually gifted adolescents, I worked for 9 years with students who engaged in cutting behavior. It was in this context that I first learned of self-injurious behavior.

The foundation of self-injury/self-expressive behavior has a few important elements. Self-expressive behaviors, while sometimes idiosyncratic (obtaining a tattoo with your loved one's name on it), are more often than not about being a part of a group. For example, some fraternities have a tradition of their membership acquiring brands of the fraternity's insignia. Some motorcycle riders wear a "one percent" tattoo, revealing their full membership in an exclusive group—the 1% of motorcyclists whose lives are very much about motorcycles (authentic bikers)—but also demonstrating a separateness from everyone outside their group. This conveys the message "I am a part of this group, but you are not." These forms of self-injury/self-expressive behaviors are at their bases tribal and public. Members are part of a small community or group that is defined by its mores, values, rules, and behaviors. Therefore, the experience of the discomfort or pain that is associated with the brands, tattoos, and so forth is necessary to becoming a part of the group—no pain, no gain. No pain, no group membership. It is important to note that the self-injurious behaviors associated with such membership rituals are not at their core due to any emotional problems or limited coping behaviors.

By contrast, cutting behavior is at its core a private act, one that is not intended as a public indication of membership in a subgroup. Cutting behaviors are intentional acts, often using knives and/or razor blades to slice the skin. Common locations for cutting include the wrists and ankles. Because society holds a taboo against self-injurious behavior, the self-inflicted wounds are typically hidden. There are sometimes exceptions to this rule, however.

Cutting behavior is inherently about the alleviation of pain. Much of the pain is private and often unknown to anyone else. An important myth about those who cut is that they are suicidal. Fox and Hawton (2004) noted that in fact, cutting behavior is an effort to obtain relief from unbearable pain. For many, cutting provides fast relief from distressing thoughts and emotions and helps the individual regain a sense of control. According to Favazza (1996), cutting has three basic purposes: (1) to distract from emotional pain or despair, (2) to dissociate from deep sadness that could lead to emotional numbness, and (3) symbolism. Cutters have reported a sense of relief when they see a flow of blood and describe the experience as regaining a sense of control.

A wide range of estimates of the prevalence rates of cutting behavior in the general population has been offered, from less than 5% to approximately 20%, but the broader category of rates of self-injury among American college students revealed a 32% rate (Vanderhoff & Lynn, 2001). Due to these wide variations, I am unwilling to offer a definitive prevalence rate. However, to gain some insight into cutting behavior especially among gifted adolescents, I interviewed Dr. Vickie Barton, coexecutive director of a residential academy for academically gifted 11th and 12th graders. As the school's lead counseling service provider, Barton estimates that for each of the past several years she has seen approximately 5% of the total student body for cutting and scratching behavior. She believes that an additional 1% or 2% of the students elude identification (V. Barton, personal communication, 2007). A prevalence rate of 5% or 6% for cutting as one form of self-injurious behavior among this sample of gifted adolescents gives us a reasonable estimate of what may be occurring in the larger gifted population.

The *DSM-IV-TR* indicated that cutting behavior/self-injury is associated with a variety of factors including borderline personality disorder, trauma, abuse, eating disorder, low self-esteem, and perfectionism. See Figure 1, Precursors to Self-Injury (LifeSIGNS, 2007), which illustrates the conditions believed to lead to cutting types of self-injurious behavior.

We know that a portion of our young people engage in myriad behaviors that can be described as self-injurious. Some of the behaviors such as tattooing and piercing are artifacts of efforts to become part of a group or to express an aspect of one's self. Others are engaging in behaviors that are more worrisome, most likely revealing evidence of distress. These behaviors include cutting. Although prevalence rates for these behaviors among the gifted child population are not readily known, it is clear that gifted students also are engaging in some, if not all, of these same behaviors. The etiology of cutting behavior, unlike tattooing and piercing, is rooted in experiences of emotional pain. Cutting seems to provide temporary solace to the person who engages in this self-injurious act.

It is important to watch for signs of emotional distress among our gifted population and to seek counseling support if there is any evidence of cutting or scratching having taken place. This particular set of behaviors requires the assistance of experts in the psychological arena and falls well outside the realm of typical patterns of social and emotional needs of gifted students. With vigilance in looking for and referring children who show evidence of these self-injurious acts, we can help them through this difficult and complicated period of their lives by providing the emotional safety net they need.

FOR DISCUSSION

- Can you imagine a student exposing his or her self-mutilation to you? What could you do to encourage such confidence? What might you do to inhibit a student from talking to you?

- Discuss the difference in motivations for self-mutilation and self-expression. How might these be different among gifted students?

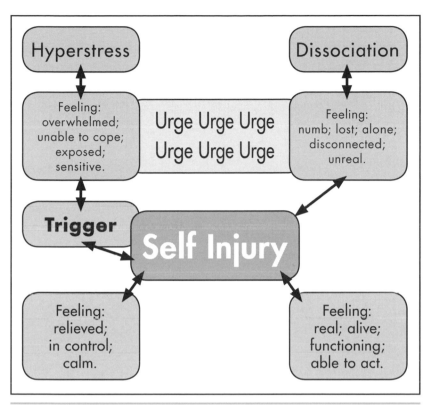

Figure 1. Precursors to Self-Injury (LifeSIGNS, 2007)

CHAPTER 18

On Preventing Suicide Among Gifted Students

- Changing terminology to affect beliefs about suicide
- Harmful myths about suicide
- Being watchful for emotional distress

Those of us who specialize in the study, service, and advocacy of students with gifts and talents occasionally encounter a student who dies by his or her own hand. Whether the child is 6 or 21, it is tragic and represents a catastrophic loss for the person's family and society at large. What perspective-changing piece of art or piece of literature will not be created? What building will remain unimagined, or what cure for cancer will go undiscovered while people suffer? The aggregate loss to society when students die unnecessarily is unfathomable. Although the need to stop potentially suicidal people is easy to acknowledge, we all too often remain on the sidelines rather than becoming a proactive force helping to prevent completed suicides. In this column I will provide the reader some ideas for becoming active agents in the lives of suicidal students with gifts and talents.

I have found over the last two decades of working on this topic that it is incumbent upon people to take stock in their personal beliefs about suicide in general and the suicide of gifted students in particular. This first step is very helpful in clarifying assumptions and prejudices that often impede people from trying to help. At the same time, erroneous assumptions are potentially harmful to the gifted student struggling with suicidal ideation. Consequently, this first step is very important in the developmental process of becoming helpful.

Changing Our Mental Model About Suicidal Behavior

In this process, it is important to understand that suicide is a mental health issue, not a legal one. As Ms. Bonnie Ball taught me, changing only one word common to our lexicon can illustrate this difference, making a big difference in our conceptual understanding. That is, substitute the word "completed" for the word "committed" when describing suicide. This change illustrates the progress made in the field of suicidology that shifts the emphasis from a legal metaphor to a health-related metaphor. The lived experience of the person is not lost in this model and the richness of the person's life is omnipresent and not immediately reduced to a mental health classification alone.

The next important conceptual shift is to eliminate any hint of responsibility that you must be able to successfully "diagnose" a potentially suicidal gifted child. Determining imminent harm by suicide requires very specialized training limited to mental health workers such as clinical psychologists and psychiatrists. Your role is very important but different. Rather than trying to determine potential suicide, you should adopt a much lower threshold called *distress*. Determining when a child is in distress is something that caring adults do every day and trained educators can be very good at doing. When you see a gifted child manifesting concerning behaviors such as worrisome drawings on his or her notebooks or class assignments, signs of depression, self-loathing, significant relationship problems, signs of drug or alcohol abuse, attempted suicides or homicides within a child's family, or when you see important changes in behavior, put your arm both literally and metaphorically around the child's shoulder and walk him or her to the school counselor or psychologist. If neither exists in your school, go to the principal, G/T coordinator, and the like. Your role is to carefully observe and refer, with an emphasis on getting the child to the right person. It is not to wait until you have absolute proof of potential suicide, but rather to act as an educated, caring professional. Once you refer the student, you can interact as part of a team who can work on behalf on the gifted child.

Resistant Myths About Suicide

Along this developmental path there are a few myths that can immobilize people, causing them to inadvertently contribute to the problem. The first one is the fear that to mention the word suicide will increase the likelihood that it will happen. This is not the case.

A second myth is that telling a person that he or she may be suicidal can lead to a manipulation of the faculty member, meaning that the worrisome behaviors that are manifest may be deliberate as strategies for attention getting. Although this may be true, it is irrelevant; looking for attention may be a legitimate cry for help. Remember to look for evidence of distress, not imminent suicide.

Another powerful myth that stymies behavior to act on behalf of gifted students is the view that once decided, suicide is inevitable. This view of inevitability can contribute to a self-fulfilling prophecy. Intervention is what we are after. Disrupting the cognition that leads to suicidal behavior is what is required. Standing on the sideline allows the suicidal ideation to continue.

Our Responsibility as Caring Professionals

After reframing suicidal completion as a mental health issue, recognizing that your role is to carefully observe, looking for signs of distress, and then dismissing myriad myths that may have held you at bay, the next expectation is to act. It is most important to accept this information, and add to it information garnered from other sources to increasingly prepare you to act. As a growing body of caring professionals, we can reduce the successful completions of suicides by working in tandem with each other's specialties. You are not going to cause a completed suicide by acting in the manner outlined, but you might get the ball rolling that prevents one or more. Remember that time is the commodity that we are trying to enhance. With every passing day under care, the life of a gifted child has a greater chance to continue.

Let us commit to continuing our professional development to the point where we feel comfortable acting when we see a gifted student in distress. Never assume that aberrant behavior is an artifact of being gifted. By learning about how to determine when a gifted child is feeling distress, we will save these children's lives. Imagine a day without any completed suicides by our students, including our gifted students.

FOR DISCUSSION

- Reflect on your comfort level in talking about suicide. Are you willing to engage a student who you believe to be in emotional distress in conversation? Why or why not?

CHAPTER 19

Gifted Students and the Adults Who Provide for Them: Lessons Learned From Terrorism

- The need to provide safe, nonprejudicial environments for gifted students
- The importance of good acts and compassion in times of tragedy
- Gifted students must be treated as people first
- The importance of regaining control when dealing with major tragedies

Every fall, approximately 300 gifted adolescents descend on the Ball State University campus to attend the Indiana Academy for Science, Mathematics, and Humanities (the Academy). The Academy is a state-funded residential school for academically gifted 11th- and 12th-grade students. It draws its students from across the state, creating a very diverse community of high-ability learners.

The students come from more than 120 high schools, and the transition for the 160 juniors new to the Academy is always difficult. The staff of the school prepares for the onset of counseling and adjustment problems, bringing to bear a great deal of expertise and commitment.

For many years, a pattern has occurred in which the earliest concerns the Academy counseling staff must attend to revolve around homesickness, minor adjustment problems, roommate concerns, and then midterms. A week before midterm examinations, the school's student life counselors, coordinator of academic guidance, and supervisor of psychoeducational services experience a rush of students expressing worries about their impending exams. The students are attended to in numerous ways to help them work through the issues concerning them. This pattern was being observed again in 2001 until the events of September 11 occurred. Immediately thereafter, the pattern of counseling needs changed. Like most Americans (and the people of many other countries), Academy students were traumatized. A big difference in 2001 was the school's ability to provide effective counseling services given the fact that the adults at the Academy were very upset as well. Shock, worry, doubt, and fear were all visible on both the students' and the adults' faces. The need to provide a safe environment for the students may have been what enabled the school to carry on and the adults to begin the healing process themselves.

Much of the next week was spent providing basic comforts to the students. Innumerable conversations among the students, students and adults, and the adults ensued. Crying was commonplace. Efforts were made to answer questions about the meaning and intention of the event. Many of our regularly scheduled classes were used to discuss the events, and a special volunteer session in the evening also was held. The students were most interested in learning more about the Middle East. Some watched news reports, but many more set out to learn about the events in other ways, so they could better understand the meaning and significance of the terrible events. The students needed to understand. They needed to know. Very few defaulted to a simplistic understanding based on ignorance or fear. The gifted students needed to know what factors were important to understanding the events of September 11.

During this time, a Fulbright Scholar from Saudi Arabia was living at the Academy. His primary goal for being there was to create a similar school in Saudi Arabia. This person's family was about to follow him to the United States when the terrorist acts occurred. Academy students and staff had grown fond of the visiting scholar, and he was becoming an accepted part of the community. He watched Western and world news reports, becoming increasingly upset and depressed as the events of September 11 were analyzed. His heart sank as it was reported that many of the parties involved were Saudis. For 6 weeks after September 11, his wife and young daughter were unable to come to the United States to join him. They were very fearful about traveling alone and about how they might be treated here.

The first Friday after the attacks, our Saudi visitor went to pray at the local mosque. Soon after arriving, numerous local preachers and ministers and one police officer arrived. They positioned themselves around the border of the building in an effort to guarantee that those in the mosque could worship freely without fear of attack. Although there was not any indication in the local community that there would have been a problem, the effort was greatly appreciated by those from the mosque, local citizens, and many of us who were living and working at the Academy. Seeing our friend suffer alongside us, while at the same time being unable to be with his family, gave the acts of terrorism a world perspective that was obvious. The considerate acts to protect worshippers at the mosque from community members, who are often maligned as being uneducated, provincial, too conservative, and even backward, illustrated the importance of good acts in a time of tragedy. It also revealed the mischaracterization of people all over the world by the media. In essence, it reminded us to look at the behavior of people when judging their character. The Academy community was keenly aware of the kind, gentle Saudi who was as negatively affected by these events as the rest of us. He came to work every day and modeled acceptance and genuine care for others. His presence at the school provided a daily reminder of the importance of being both compassionate and knowledgeable.

The month following September 11 was very difficult for those living and working at this special residential school. When one considers that all of our students move away from their families to live together, along with the fact that the events were still very disturbing to adults months later, and will likely become an important emotional milestone for the remainder of our lives, it was a time for lessons to be learned—learned without the impediments of prejudices or preformed dispositions for how to understand the social and emotional needs of gifted students in our care. As I participated in this community, I tried to be as aware of the interactions among the various groups as possible. I also worked to help orchestrate additional assistance for any person who needed it. Perhaps more importantly, I was constantly facing evidence that supported or contradicted certain aspects of the research literature based on the social and emotional needs of gifted students.

Lessons Learned From Terrorism

As has been said many times in the past by caregivers, gifted students must be treated as children first. In our case, however, I will expand that notion by saying that gifted students must be treated as *people* first, the primary distinction here being that caring for a person is less fraught with age-specific prejudices than the notion of caring for a child. Academically gifted high-school-aged students can have very powerful intellects. They also can be as emotionally mature or immature as any of their nongifted peers. Hence, to provide for them as a caregiver in the social and emotional domain, these issues must be considered. In other words, dealing only with the human needs, or the human needs in concert with perceived personality or emotional issues taken into consideration, are inadequate strategies. This is especially true when one considers the next issue.

The behavior of the students in the aftermath of the attacks on the World Trade Center has reaffirmed for me that many gifted students have a need to understand complicated matters. Aspects of this include the need to understand matters in a thorough and multifaceted way. Other aspects of this need are issues associated with engagement and control. For some, being engaged in the pursuit of understanding is an important part of who they are as a person, and denying them that way of understanding the world is ineffectual counseling practice and potentially harmful in its own right.

Regaining a sense of control when dealing with major tragedies is important to many gifted adolescents. Although many professionals who provide counseling services for victims of trauma would say this is true for all people, it can be a little different for intellectually gifted students. For example, regaining a sense of control for many gifted students is affected by the extent to which they are allowed or encouraged to pursue a complicated understanding of matters in an intellectual way. Those providing services in times of tragedy should give gifted students opportunities to approach the healing process in this manner. To not do so can exacerbate feelings of helplessness and the sense of loss of control.

We also learned from monitoring community interactions since September 11 that this form of suffering can bring a community closer together. Interactions have been improved by the connections made by the students and adults during this time of struggle. Whether a person was adult or student, American or Saudi, local resident or Academy community member, was less important than the fact that terrorism affects virtually all people negatively. This is true because people are far more similar than not. Subsequent to the terrorist acts, some of the socially constructed barriers were dropped or relaxed, enabling better and more profound types of communications to go on. I suspect we witnessed and participated in a more raw and genuine form of existence as a community than is typically experienced. We dealt with each other as people first.

Even with the intervention efforts, a significant downside was seen. Following these events, a higher than average number of our students went back home to finish their high school experience. Although it is disappointing for our school to lose these students, we appreciate that their physical safety and emotional needs may have to be met among their families. Abraham Maslow's hierarchical theory of needs seems as viable today as ever. Our Saudi visitor's family did make it to the Academy and lifetime friendships were forged in the wake of tragedy. As this tragedy taught us, dealing with all people as human beings first, then applying appropriate counseling services based on the needs of the individual is a practice that holds great promise for guiding the social and emotional development of gifted students.

FOR DISCUSSION

- As a teacher or counselor, did your experiences of helping children following the September 11 tragedy mirror those of the children at the Academy? If not, how were they different?

- As a teacher and/or parent, do you have the school services available to deal with tragedies appropriate for the needs of gifted students?

SECTION 3

Gifted Children Today

A recurring theme in my efforts to learn more about gifted children is how different the times in which they are growing up are from my own experiences. As I have tried to evaluate their behavior and their social and emotional needs, it comes up again and again. AIDS, MTV, guns in school, the Internet—all of these impact the lives of gifted children.

I begin to explore these ideas in "Gifted Students' Social and Emotional Development in the 21st Century." Rollo May's notion that we cannot truly understand something until we have experienced it serves as a reminder to us all that we must delve ever more deeply into the psyche of young people if we want to help them succeed in these new, very different times.

In "Technology and the Unseen World of Gifted Students," I explore the use of computers with gifted students. Using Erikson's theory of psychosocial development, I also consider how engaging in various communication technologies could positively affect a gifted child's identity. The chapter that follows, "Digital Immigrants, Natives, and 'Tweeners': A Glimpse Into the Future for Our Students With Gifts and Talents," discusses the growing generation of students comfortable with technologies to a point far beyond many of the adults in their lives. "Nerds and Geeks: Society's Evolving Stereotypes of Our Students With Gifts and Talents," the next chapter, discusses how the vernacular surrounding academic achievement and intelligence has changed for society at large.

The chapters that follow also deal with many realities of gifted students' lives. The tragic incident at Columbine High School in April of 1999 is a most potent indicator of the different times in which these children are growing up. How giftedness plays a role in their experience is the emphasis of the chapter titled "The Lived Experiences of Gifted Students in School, or On Gifted Students and Columbine." Building on the concepts discussed in the first section ("About Gifted Children: Who They Are and Why"), this chapter explores misconceptions about gifted children and how they interact with these new times to make an even more complicated world for gifted young people.

In "The Rage of Gifted Students," I examine the various layers of influence on gifted students' experiences and the ways these influences may generate feelings of rage in these individuals. I conclude this chapter with suggestions for how we can help gifted students reduce or eliminate their feelings of rage.

Another aspect of the social milieu of schools is discussed in "The Many Faces of Bullies." Gifted students are growing up in a world filled with many real and perceived threats to their physical and social safety. Appreciating the historical context in which gifted students live is an important step in guiding their social and emotional development.

The final chapter in this section, "Psychological Autopsy Provides Insight Into Gifted Adolescent Suicide," was created from my research into gifted adolescent suicide. This chapter is a synopsis of the findings of a study my colleagues, Robert Cook and David Dixon, and I conducted on the lives of three adolescents who committed suicide. The detailed descriptions of these adolescents and their circumstances were developed through a psychological autopsy process. Learning about these students led us to the development of specific recommendations for preventing suicides of gifted adolescents. I cannot emphasize enough the need to be on the lookout for indicators of suicidal behavior and the need to be proactive, no matter how uncomfortable it may be. Professional counselors are key in the solution to the destructive notions these adolescents hold, but they can do nothing if adults are not aware of the need for their intervention.

CHAPTER 20

Gifted Students' Social and Emotional Development in the 21st Century

KEY CONCEPTS

- Generational influences on psychosocial development
- To know something, one must experience it (idea from Rollo May)
- Global economy's influence on psychosocial development

The complications involved in raising children increased significantly during the second half of the 20th century. Charles Dickens's famous line, "It was the best of times, it was the worst of times," from his novel *A Tale of Two Cities*, seems an apt statement to describe societal changes since 1960. These changes have been so dramatic and pervasive that they are, in fact, hard to fully comprehend. The last 40 years have seen many changes, from what were once considered global issues, such as population growth and environmental concerns (seemingly so distant and unrelated to those of us living in the United States 40 years ago), to the daily activities in which we each engage. As we guide today's youth, we must consider both the broad and specific contexts of our children's times. In the last 40 years, we have moved from only three available television channels to literally hundreds, from curable types of venereal diseases to herpes and AIDS, from 16k of computer memory to terabytes at roughly the same cost, and from letter writing to e-mail, and the world's population has grown from three billion to six billion people.

Given the important ways in which our world has changed and will continue to change, those of us who grew up in earlier generations need to appreciate that we can only know *about* what it is like to be growing up gifted in the new millennium. Despite the breadth and depth of the changes, one might argue that small-town life has not changed much over the past 40 years. Although this can be a true statement, I would note that MTV is one example of how a generation has been connected through image and sound, unlike all previous generations. This one simple example brings to bear all of the considerations associated with psychosocial development. For example, historically, as a young child moved from his or her parents being the ones with the greatest influence on his or her immediate behavior to friends being more influential, the small groups of friends tended to carefully reflect the child's immediate communities in terms of values, appearance, and conduct. Via MTV and other similar channels, today's young people make a visual and auditory connection with youth throughout the United States. Consequently, the reference groups of youth are no longer so closely tied to immediate communities. Issues such as fitting in, developing a peer group, and understanding one's role in his or her family and the broader culture are but a few of the issues that emerge to influence the needs of gifted children. All of these concerns and experiences occur as children are forming their identities.

The following are two examples of ways that children's experiences vary significantly from those of previous generations and illustrate meaningful variations within the past 20 years.

Schooling practices have gone from:

◈ textbooks and worksheets to computers,

◈ teacher-directed to students-as-teachers, and

◈ classroom lectures to students becoming responsible for the construction of their own learning through processes of inquiry.

Access to information has gone from:

◈ slow and sometimes unattainable to immediate and overwhelming,

◈ being out in the world collecting information to collecting information from home, and

◈ collecting information manually to relying on computers.

As adults, we must realize that, while we try to understand our children's lives, in many important ways they are unlike our own. A famous psychologist, Rollo May (1969), wrote that we must recognize the difference between knowing *about* something and truly knowing something. May described how he came down with tuberculosis and was on his deathbed. He dealt with the salient aspects and issues of preparing for death. He recovered and came to realize that, before this experience, he only knew about death. After having experienced the life of a dying person, he truly knew death. To know something, one must experience it. Most of our lives are spent merely knowing about things. As newborns, we learn in a prelingual manner largely determined by our parents until our mobility allows for our own experimentation. Even with trial and error experiences, we are being taught to learn vicariously by watching and listening to others. We also learn how to create and understand the world as mental activities without relying on others' input or examples.

Much of what we come to know about and believe comes from our environmental teachings and mental constructions, and far less through our own experiments. This distinction is important for many reasons. The first is that no two people can have the exact same understanding of any situation or construct. Another is that historical analysis has taught us that cohorts in history often reveal patterns of thought and value formations that are similar. For example, in the United States, the young adult population living during the Watergate scandal has maintained a level and type of political skepticism different from those of the young adults of the Reagan era. A third is that, along with the acceleration of technological advances over the past 40 years, there has been tremendous growth in the knowledge of virtually all subjects. Various means, such as the Internet and personal computers, now provide access to the expanding information base in increasingly easier and faster ways. There now exists a "digital divide," a serious and expanding gap among the knowledge, opportunities, and wealth of those in the world who have regular and easy access to this information and those who have neither.

The relationship between young children's access to self-selected material and their social and emotional development has yet to be studied. Therefore, it is difficult to predict the effects on typical development patterns in young children of the immediate access to and consumption of material that cuts across topics and age appropriateness.

Another major confluence of events radically changing current experiences (and hence all that is affected by them) is the movement to a world economy. Opportunities and expectations are becoming influenced by what is and is not perceived as possible. For example, many Indiana natives who grew up between the 1950s and the 1980s aspired to and relied on manufacturing jobs upon graduation from high school. This possibility allowed families to remain physically close and often work together. In recent years, however, the move to a world economy has drained the manufacturing jobs that once defined the state's economy. Despite the fact that the state has relatively low unemployment rates of 4%–5%, the adult population is often underemployed and earns a fourth to a third of their previous incomes, while their children grapple with giving up on their aspirations. This evolution is slow and often painful. More importantly, these changes are being played out on a world stage where being a consumer is characterized as being a good citizen.

As concerned adults interested in helping the psychosocial development of gifted students, we should first heed Rollo May's words: To truly know and understand another's experiences, we must live them ourselves. Secondly, we should maintain a healthy respect for those experiences consistent across generations and those that are not. We must be aware of the differences in children's experiences and in our own. With our new appreciation for the profound differences of experience, we should draw on all resources available to assist our children. It also would be helpful for adults to learn some basic theory about human development, particularly as it pertains to the psychosocial development of gifted students. There are certain aspects of human development theory that are resistant to change over time.

By realizing our limitations in being truly empathetic to others' experiences and by utilizing the strategies noted above, we have the opportunity to provide effective guidance to the gifted youth of the 21st century. I am sure that Rollo May, by asking us to experience another's suffering in order to know it, never meant to encourage the pain and suffering of even one additional person in order to widen expertise in the face of any specific tragedy. I am quite confident that he would have advised us to operate in a climate of trust and with an appreciation for the child's experiences as meaningful and valid. Our role should, therefore, be one of compassion and respect for the uniqueness of all gifted children as they struggle with the development of their identity while on the path to self-actualization.

FOR DISCUSSION

- Provide two further examples of how gifted children's experiences today differ from those of previous generations.

- What strategies (as mentioned in previous chapters) do you think would be most effective in dealing with generational or global influences on gifted individuals' psychological development?

CHAPTER 21

Technology and the Unseen World of Gifted Students

- Gifted students' experiences with computer-based communications technologies fall into four categories: freedom of expression, control, power, and feeling connected
- Erikson's theory of psychosocial development
- The positive influences of technology on Eriksonian crises

The social and emotional development of gifted students can be influenced by many factors. Genetics, experiences, learning, family values, perceptions, and interactions all contribute to the development of gifted children. Under the heading of experiences is students' use of computers. This chapter will highlight some of the uses of computers by gifted students. The potential effects of using these technologies will be discussed using two stages of Erikson's theory of psychosocial development as a framework.

For almost two decades, children have had increasing opportunities to use computers. Many homes now have one or more computers, and virtually all schools in the United States have at least one. It is also common for schools to have one or more computer labs and classroom computers. For example, the Indiana Academy for Science, Mathematics, and Humanities provides every student a laptop computer with wireless Internet access. Student access to personal computers has clearly been enhanced over the past 20 years.

Times also have changed in terms of the nature of the personal computers to which students have access. Technology has changed from the early days (circa 1982) of home computers with 16k of memory and no hard drive, to today's multiple gigahertz dual processors and numerous inexpensive, yet powerful peripherals. Students often have cell phones at earlier ages than before, with many of these being smartphones capable of browsing the Internet. Other devices like iPods, iPads, tablets, and electronic readers also allow students to utilize online capabilities, word processing programs, games, and communication software. The evolution in the technological capacity of computers and mobile devices parallels the growing options available to students. For example, just imagine the difference between the original game of *Pong* and newer strategy games. A similar evolution of opportunity and impact on students exists as the Internet has evolved. After word processing, the first and most common use of computers is electronic mail (e-mail). Online gaming and social networking are also very popular among children.

When trying to understand the development of our gifted children interfacing with computer-based communication technologies, we can only speculate. At this point in history, very little research exists that attempts to address the questions listed below. Consequently, this chapter is based more on my observations and experiences running a residential high school for academically gifted students and, to a small degree, involvement with my own children.

Four Types of Communications Technologies

E-Mail

People of all ages and backgrounds use e-mail to communicate with others. Prior communication issues associated with time and distance are easily surpassed using this technology. Messages can be sent with or without attachments. Pictures and even full-motion video can be passed from one person to another around the world requiring very little time. For example, a baby can be born in Houston, TX, at 3 a.m., and minutes later grandparents in Hawaii can download and print pictures of the newborn child. These opportunities, while recent additions to adults' lives (over the past 20 years), are commonplace to today's children. This means that our children are growing up with a greater facility for computer-based technologies than their parents, a fact that should not be underappreciated.

Instant Messaging and Texting

Instant messaging (in some ways a more limited form of e-mail) is quite common today, with students communicating with multiple "buddies" at one time in real time. Because of technological enhancements, these interactions can go on while other computer activities are being carried out. It is similar to being on the telephone, but users can talk and send typed messages over the Internet to many people at once. Increasingly, students are using this communications technology while doing homework. In the same vein, students use texting via smartphones or cell phones to share short messages and photos. In essence, instant messaging and texting allow gifted students separated by varying distances to communicate with one another instantly while engaging in other activities.

Chat Rooms and Social Networking

Chat rooms tend to be made up of people with some interest in common. They communicate often without knowing the other people with whom they are "chatting." The chat rooms range from being relatively public to being extremely private. One's involvement may be a single event, a regular pattern, or an ongoing compulsion. Similarly, social networking allows students to interact with "friends" they've only met online (and those they know in person) via sites like Facebook, MySpace, and Twitter. As with chat rooms, participation on social networking sites can range from very private conversations to public displays of photos, upcoming events, or back-and-forth dialogue.

Online Diaries or Journals (Blogs)

The final example is online diaries or journals, also called weblogs or blogs. Online journals, which are set up through websites, can take many forms. Some are relatively confidential, with only chosen outsiders able to view the "blogged" materials. At the opposite end of the continuum are journals open to everyone. Details revealed in this form of communication run the gamut from relatively innocuous information to descriptions of the most personal kind.

Erikson's Theory of Psychosocial Development

Before highlighting salient parts of the experience of engaging with other people through these forms of technology, I want to use Erik Erikson's (1963) theory of psychosocial development to provide some parameters. His theory is important because it establishes a framework for understanding the typical psychosocial developmental patterns in people. A second important feature of Erikson's theory is its claim that a person's id is free from internal conflict, but susceptible in its development to psychosocial conflict, and not internal psychosexual conflict, as Freud had claimed. Erikson believed that conflict arises from a person's interaction with his or her environment, not merely the internal forces of the person. Consequently, the culture in which a person lives is important to his or her psychosocial development, a position I have espoused for 20 years.

Erikson's theory includes eight developmental stages. During each stage, a crisis must be resolved in order for a person to develop further without carrying forward issues tied to the previous crises. During the infancy stage (first year of life), Erikson posits that the primary crisis to be resolved is one of trust versus mistrust. He described the task to be resolved during the second year of life (toddler) as autonomy versus shame and doubt. The preschooler stage (years 3–5) includes initiative versus guilt as the primary crisis. The elementary school stage includes competence versus inferiority as the crisis to be resolved. Adolescence is the period when the individual must refine his or her sense of identity or struggle with role confusion. During early adulthood, intimacy versus isolation is the crisis to be resolved. Generativity or despair is the crisis to be resolved during middle adulthood. The final developmental crisis was called integrity versus despair.

According to Erikson, as the individual negotiates a crisis at each stage of development, a basic strength or virtue emerges. He described eight basic virtues that he believed emerge across a person's psychosocial development: hope, will, purpose, competence, fidelity, love, care, and wisdom, respectively. Because this chapter focuses on school-aged children, only the third (competence versus inferiority) and fourth (identity versus role confusion) psychosocial crises will be discussed.

Experiences and Benefits

The following is a list of experiences and benefits that I feel comfortable reporting as part of using computer-based communications technologies. Generally speaking, the experience of using e-mail, instant messaging, chat rooms, and online diaries falls into four major categories: freedom of expression, control, power, and feeling connected. Each of these four also contains nuances that vary across people. For example, for some gifted students, freedom of expression includes a greater sense of empowerment rooted in the immediacy and control of the expression; it can also serve as a catharsis. Others experience feelings of excitement and joy to have convenient outlets for expression when they perceive that adults (parents and teachers) control much of their lives. Remaining anonymous when communicating can create feelings of safety and power. Crossing age groups often creates feelings of being adult-like, as well as a sense of rebelliousness. Other feelings associated with using these forms of technologies include privacy, immediacy, ownership, imagination, freedom, utility, and feelings of belonging that come from participating with others of similar interest. Perhaps the greatest experience that comes from these forms of interaction is a greater sense of connectedness and, therefore, acceptance. Many gifted children have commented on their surprise at finding other people "like me" through these types of interactions.

With the experiences and benefits made possible using these forms of computer-based communications technologies, what are the ramifications for the social and emotional development of gifted students relative to Erikson's third (competence versus inferiority) and fourth (identity versus role confusion) crises of development? Although it is too early to tell and there is far too little research currently available, we can say that we are immersed in a culture wherein these kinds of technological interactions are increasingly common to our young gifted population. It is reasonable to assume that these behaviors will increase to the point where future generations of gifted students have a large portion of their relationships created in this virtual world. It is easy to see positive potential in the development of competence in the use of these technologies. For example, communicating with others via technology requires a modest degree of skill. Typing, navigating the Internet, word processing, composing, analyzing, and generally expressing one's thoughts and feelings are skills that can be enhanced using these forms of communication. All of these examples are indicative of skills that can lead to an increasing sense of agency and positive self-concept.

We can imagine how the experiences and benefits of engaging in these communication technologies could positively affect a gifted child's identity. Outlets for expression that allow for valued interactions with others, provide information, and build relationships are important to the development of one's identity. Arguably, the most important benefit of using computer-based communications to interact with others is the feeling of being connected (part of a community) and gaining a sense of belonging. From those feelings, acceptance is often the next step of development to emerge. It is very important in the lives of gifted students to feel accepted. This allows them to move forward in life not feeling aberrant or detached from society. Moreover, as Erikson described in his theory, several virtues can develop as the crises are resolved. The virtues he proposes are, therefore, potentially tied to the benefits of the students' use of these communications technologies. These experiences and benefits can assist in resolving the crises at the two stages of development discussed, potentially influencing the emergence of the virtues of hope, will, purpose, and competence.

If these Eriksonian crises can be positively affected by the use of these technologies, why do adults carry around so much worry and concern about (gifted) children using technology? Most adults did not grow up with access to computers and therefore do not have the facility for, or comfort level with, using them in place of other communications tools. A second reason is that the adults' role in the children's upbringing can seem diminished when they cannot directly participate with the children. There is a great fear of the unknown, and many adults' worries are enhanced due to the media's portrayal of some children being exploited at the hands of some unscrupulous Internet users. In a nutshell, many adults' unfamiliarity with computers causes them to feel cautious and somewhat impotent toward technological communications.

Unanswered Questions

The social and emotional development of gifted children is clearly being affected by the use of these communication technologies. How they are being affected is only now beginning to emerge. Below I have listed numerous unanswered questions about how the use of these computer-based communications technologies affects gifted students' social and emotional development.

◈ What are the effects on the social and emotional development of gifted students from encounters with others they do not see? For example, what are the effects on their identity formation, friendship formation, and issues of self?

◈ What are the effects of short- and long-term interactions when anonymity is ever-present among some or all of the participants?

◈ What are the effects of new relationships and friendships emerging from these modes of communication?

◈ How does building relationships using these technologies translate back into school?

◈ How does building relationships using these technologies affect the third (competence versus inferiority) and fourth (identity versus role confusion) crises of Erikson's theory?

❖ What direction can be provided to adults about the use of communications technologies in raising and teaching gifted students?

As with most aspects of guiding the social and emotional development of gifted students, until these questions are answered, it is important that we stay involved with our children and use common sense about setting limitations and providing safety for them. We also need to support our children's interests and learn about them to the fullest extent we can. Having faith in them, while at the same time realizing that they are children, is always good advice. And, some time in the near future, answers to these questions will provide additional guidance for us as we attempt to guide our gifted students' social and emotional development.

FOR DISCUSSION

A number of unanswered questions were put forward. Select and discuss a question that you consider important:

- What are the effects on the social and emotional development of gifted students of encounters with others they do not see? For example, what are the effects on their identity formation, friendship formation, and issues of self?

- What are the effects of short- and long-term interactions when anonymity is ever-present among some or all of the participants?

- What are the effects of new relationships and friendships emerging from these modes of communication?

- How does building relationships using these technologies translate back into school?

- How does building relationships using these technologies affect the third (competence versus inferiority) and fourth (identity versus role confusion) crises of Erikson's theory?

- What direction can be provided to adults about the use of communications technologies in raising and teaching gifted students?

CHAPTER 22

Digital Immigrants, Natives, and "Tweeners": A Glimpse Into the Future for Our Students With Gifts and Talents

- Changing cultures
- Digital natives, digital immigrants, and tweeners
- The importance of technology to young people's lives
- Digital immigrants and the clock on the VCR

Among the many important changes occurring across the world is the movement to make all electronic products digitally based. This digital revolution means that most forms of technology will soon have the same basic architecture, allowing communication across computers, cameras, telephones, and so forth. Through wires, memory chips, and wireless technologies, technology (and therefore humans) are starting to communicate with the same basic language. It appears that in a short period of time, all forms of technology will "speak the same language."

Speaking the same technological language exists within the larger digital culture much like speaking a language is part of any other culture. To function fully in any culture, one must speak the language. When schools attempt to teach a second language, cultural aspects are used to provide a semi-immersion experience for the student. It is widely known that, to become fluent in a second language, one should spend time immersed in that culture.

In 2010, virtually everyone in the U.S. over the age of 30 or so has become an immigrant in their own country—digital immigrants. In this definition, being an immigrant means being new to the digital culture, not knowing of or understanding the nuances on which a culture is built. In essence, this large group of Americans is really bicultural.

Where there are cultural (digital) immigrants, there must be cultural (digital) natives (Prensky, 2001). Being a digital native suggests that one has grown up immersed in a culture so that its nuances are accessible to the person, not foreign or unintelligible, make sense, and can be inferred. An early hint that this change to a technological culture was coming could be seen in an unassuming little test—the setting of the clock on the VCR. The dichotomous experience of being one who comfortably sets the clock as compared to those who could not, or would not, foreshadowed things to come. Whether one is a digital native or immigrant today is representative of a complicated relationship of understanding a culture—the culture of digital technology.

These changes provide a background for the following observations and questions, which illustrate changes that have occurred and/or are on the horizon. Some of the ramifications for students with gifts and talents are also noted.

My first observation is that there is a third category to add to the digital native and immigrant dictionary. That is the "tweeners," those who have qualities of both groups. For example, among my wife's and my four children, who range in age from 16–22 years, we witness on a daily basis skills, attitudes, and interests that could be placed on a continuum of digital immersion. This is in contrast to the proposed dichotomy of natives and immigrants. Our 22-year-old twins grew up with computers and are quite computer savvy, using digital technology much of each day. However, it does not define them as much as seems to be the case for our younger two children, aged 16 and 19 years. They are both more knowledgeable about and interested in technology in all its forms. They speak digital speak and engage in digital manipulation of memory transfer across forms of technology. They carry iPods and cell phones, constantly transferring memory between them. They use the telephone for music and photography, as well as its original intent. The list of how they manipulate technology is endless. So while all four children are technically savvy and digitally literate, only two are seemingly representative of the digital native category. The two older children are "tweeners," in that they walk relatively comfortably among two cultures to the extent and in the manner to which they care.

Some Unanswered Questions

Although the following questions are appropriate for all students, please ask yourself when reading them, "What does this mean for students with gifts and talents today?"

1. How does this evolution in technology affect the children of today, given the wide range in level of access to it?
2. What does digital technology hold for the future, relative to access to information, other people, and the like?
3. How does a technology that emphasizes the culture of oneself ("the culture of me") going to impact the moral and ethical development of the youth of today?
4. What will the movement toward digital technology becoming transparent to us mean for each of these groups?
5. Can digital technology become a means to break down the financial barriers that exist across our public schools?
6. What does all this mean for those of us who never quite mastered that clock on the VCR? Are we doomed to see a flashing 12:00 for the rest of our lives?

A Few Observations

I have noted in the past how the terms *nerd* and *geek*, typically used as disparaging descriptors of gifted and talented students, have evolved over the past 20 years, becoming less pejorative and more descriptive. That gifted student who plans to "be nerdy tonight and stay at home and study" is an example. The shift to the current meaning of nerd and geek is somewhat associated with the emergence of computers in our daily lives. As a consequence, increasing numbers of children have developed interests and skills in computers and as such communicate about them regularly. This has led to an acceptance of students with gifts and talents who have passions in this area. As the digital revolution unfolds, an unintended byproduct, as driven by the vast numbers of students of all abilities using digital technologies, may become the most powerful change agent known to improve the social acceptance of students with gifts and talents. The students with gifts and talents will become more accepted into the mainstream by the vast majority of students due to the similar (digital) language being common to the group. Where they were once outsiders to mainstream culture, they will be speaking the same language and sharing the nuances of the digital culture. Those of us over 30, however, may become the outsiders once again—destined to watch as the VCR blinks 12:00 forever.

FOR DISCUSSION

- Do you think your comfort or discomfort with technology affects your interactions with students with gifts and talents?

- How might the digital revolution be beneficial to students with gifts and talents?

- Do you expect all students with gifts and talents to be proficient with technology? What might be the effects of such an expectation?

CHAPTER 23

Nerds and Geeks: Society's Evolving Stereotypes of Our Students With Gifts and Talents

KEY CONCEPTS

- Perceptions about the gifted are changing
- Expanding acceptability

Over the past 25 years, my colleagues and I have conducted research into the experiences of our students with gifts and talents, particularly those in school. We have written many papers and even a couple of books describing these students' lives and how they live them. An obvious part of their experience can be reflected in the stereotypes used in society to describe these children. The two most common ones are *nerd* and *geek*. When we first started interviewing gifted students about these terms in 1982, we found that both terms had very negative ramifications in the gifted students' perceptions. For example, nerds were generally considered as socially inadequate, shy or overbearing, smart, and perhaps *too* smart, as we learned later in our studies. Nerds also were perceived as being very focused on academic endeavors, physically weak, uninteresting, unnecessary to society, and ultimately undesirable. Generally speaking, all of these things might be categorized under the heading of feeling abhorred, which was the way most of these students described their experience of being gifted.

Although the term *nerd* had many negative connotations, the term *geek* was even more potent. Some students I met years ago in programs that I have championed or been director of had in a way reconciled themselves to being thought of as nerdy, but they really did not want to be thought of as geeks. Geek was a term that at that time had great power to stigmatize. The experience of being a geek was as one who others are embarrassed to be around. This element of guilt by association is an important component of the stigma theory of Erving Goffman (1963). Geeks were thought to be extremely inadequate socially—more so than the nerds—and also too focused in academic or technical endeavors.

Starting in the early 1980s, many popular films, books, and television shows have been produced with an intellectually capable student as the main character. Some examples are *Searching for Bobby Fischer* (1993); *Good Will Hunting* (1997); and *Family Matters* (1989–1997), a sitcom that showcased teenager Steve Urkel as "America's favorite nerd." All of these examples portrayed gifted students in a broader light than did the strict stereotypes that were just described. Even though these characters did have some negative aspects to their lives that were tied to society's stereotypes, they were seen as people—as individuals—and that was a huge step forward.

As the years passed, the current generation of children has grown up immersed in an increasingly rich technological society. This continues today with many homes having computers of one form or another. In general, children are receiving a significant amount of exposure to media of different kinds, and thus also have gained experience in using many diverse technologies (e.g., video games, smartphones, PDAs). Because of this exposure, this generation of children who are now in their teens has become so technologically savvy that being passionate about technology is becoming more commonplace, an emerging norm of sorts. This passion for technology has not only improved children's learning experiences, but also has had a dramatic effect on the term *geek*.

The term *geek* is now used increasingly as an adjective, rather than merely a strict stereotype. For example, "tech geek" is a common phrase used to describe someone whose passion for technology has made him or her a computer expert. This more positive spin on the word has occurred for two reasons. First, many people in our society are passionate about computers, so being viewed as an expert is socially rewarding. Second, because many others strive to become more technologically savvy, the expert or geek is seen as a helper, and in many cases the term *geek* even attaches an avant-garde quality to this individual. In addition to the individual striving to become more technologically advanced, the evolution of cyber cafés and other multimedia advances in our culture (especially in bigger cities), have contributed to the evolving stereotype of a geek.

So, where does this leave us in the year 2010? What does this mean, and what does this suggest for gifted kids? Well, in listening carefully, interviewing, and observing gifted children, I have learned that the term *nerd* has become rather neutral. It has almost become like a color in certain ways it is used. It is as though a person can be nerdy but also have many other qualities that are not included under that stereotype from 25 years ago. I believe that people like Bill Gates and other figures who present themselves in ways that would historically have placed them in the category of a nerd or a geek are no longer viewed as such because of the extent to which our society holds these people in such reverence. This societal perception also has had a large impact on the way our cultural stereotypes for nerds and geeks have evolved.

Obviously, as a psychologist who studies gifted children, I am pleased that these terms are losing their negative power. I think there will be many benefits as the terms get increasingly fleshed out and used more neutrally. Recently, I overheard young gifted children using the term *nerd* in the following way: "I am going to be nerdy today and stay at home and work on my homework." This statement implies that being a nerd is actually a choice, not a state of being. This semantic distinction between choosing a behavior and manifesting negatively perceived traits is important to stigma theory because behavior is changeable, while attributing negatives to another's appearance is merely an attribution that is socially influenced. As evidence of this evolution in the stereotype, the term *geek* also is often used in very specific ways such as being a tech geek, or a geek for art, news, or weather. What is interesting and worth noting about these changes is their similarity to another analogy: the swan emerging from an ugly duckling. Being thought of as a nerd as a child (an ugly duckling) does not have the negative connotation that it once did. The knowledge of what great things can come from such early interests (the swan) has motivated a change in perceptions of the "nerdy" child. Therefore, the accoutrements to being academically oriented or working hard in school, in time, could cease to be as problematic for children in our schools as before.

Our schools have been described as anti-intellectual environments by many people in the field of gifted education including Howley, Howley, and Pendarvis (1995) and Coleman and Cross (2001). However, the evolution in these two stereotypes suggests that there is a growing awareness of the importance of competence in our society. This realization represents our society's movement from a manufacturing base to an information age. Our children are seeing this, and the change has primarily focused on the recognition that people like Bill Gates (once considered to be a geek) make very significant contributions to our society, and other intellectually gifted individuals are handsomely rewarded for their accomplishments. Thus, the children who would have been typically identified early by their peers as a nerd or geek, and experienced the stigma of giftedness (Coleman & Cross, 1988) and limited social acceptance (Cross, Coleman, & Terhaar-Yonkers, 1991), are now less likely to experience being an outcast. This is due to the growing awareness that being a nerd or geek could actually have a positive outcome. I am encouraged to think that these students' experiences in life will improve in a parallel fashion as the use of these two terms and stereotypes evolve. Perhaps one day these gifted students will be able to live without the negative social consequences associated with being a student with gifts and talents.

I have often said that one of the great outcomes of Western society's integration of computers has been to remind us that children are far more capable than adults often give them credit for being. As adults, many of us who are computer immigrants rely on our children—or children in general—to be our advisers because they have a higher degree of facility and expertise than we have, or will ever have. This transference of skills from child to adult is yet another mechanism that is assisting in the evolution of these stereotypes and also has the potential to improve the lives of gifted students. Perhaps things will improve enough that one day I will have inscribed on my gravestone "He aspired to be a geek."

FOR DISCUSSION

- Do you believe that students with gifts and talents are becoming better accepted among their peers? Why or why not?

- What can adults do to encourage a more favorable attitude?

CHAPTER 24

The Lived Experiences of Gifted Students in School, or On Gifted Students and Columbine

KEY CONCEPTS

- Stigma of Giftedness Paradigm
- Idiosyncratic patterns of development
- Gifted students deal with mixed messages at a micro level and macro level in school

---

The purpose of this chapter is to create a context for understanding gifted students' lives in school. To that end, I will highlight how gifted students deal with the mixed messages they perceive from their environment and try to make a connection with these messages to the tragedy at Columbine High School in 1999. Although the topic is quite somber, there is ultimately good news to be shared about gifted students' lives.

Since the mid-1980s, Larry Coleman and I have been publishing research about the lives of gifted students in school (e.g., Coleman & Cross, 1988; Cross et al., 1991). Data for some of the early articles published on this topic were collected during evaluations of schools and programs for gifted students. During the early evaluations (circa 1984), the gifted students described in great detail what their lives in their local schools were "really like." The "really like" aspect of their comments inspired us to approach the research in a more serious, deliberate, and focused manner. Since then Larry and I, individually and in tandem, have gathered data from thousands of gifted students in grades K–12 from numerous states across the nation. We have used surveys and questionnaires; made observations; interviewed students, teachers, parents, and administrators; visited numerous schools and classrooms; and read students' journals—all in the quest of understanding gifted students' lives in school. Over the past 20 years, we have published approximately 60 articles and presented more than 110 papers together at conferences dealing with gifted students. The research has led me to my ideas about the shootings at Columbine. This chapter will provide ideas that were developed while I worked on the various studies previously reported. In addition to this line of research, I have increasingly focused on the psychology of gifted students, with a specialization in the suicidal behaviors of gifted students. Our research into the social and emotional development of gifted students, their experiences of giftedness, their social cognition, and their social coping strategies and behaviors also have helped inform this chapter.

For 20 years, I have claimed that schools are first and foremost a social enterprise where some academic learning goes on. Although I have used this statement to frame my social-cognitive orientation, the original idea emerged during an interview with a gifted adolescent who was describing to me his life as a student. The detail reflected in his perceptions about the expectations within his school was most impressive. He also described expectations from outside his school that reflect messages society held about gifted students. The degree to which the messages were mixed was quite astonishing to me. For example, he received the message that gifted students are physically weak, socially inadequate, and not interesting people. They are out of touch, unattractive, and have a high propensity for mental problems. Although the student knew that many of these descriptors did not fit him, he had come to believe that being labeled as gifted was somewhat limiting. Another important message he received was that going to college was important. To go to college, one needs to work hard as a student. He also believed that pursuing excellence was important in life. For example, "do your best" was the single most frequent comment he received from adults.

Across these various messages was a thread that established implicit parameters on his behavior that was different than the messages. The thread was interpreted as *not too*. Study hard, but *not too* hard. Pursue academic passions, but *not too* much. Even do your best in school, but *not* if it means spending *too* much time or energy to do so. Increasingly, the understood message was that, to be a healthy person, one spreads time spent in activities across a variety of endeavors that seem reasonable to adults. A secondary message inferred from these mixed messages was that being gifted should not take too much time or, said differently, if one must spend so much time on his or her academic studies, then he or she must not be gifted.

Over the years, I have heard other beliefs held by many gifted students that pertain to these mixed messages. Three of the most common are the following:

◆ that others hold expectations about gifted students;

◆ that if one becomes known as a gifted student, it affects how others treat him or her; and

◆ that one learns that if he or she can manage the information others gain about him or her, then he or she can maintain more social latitude.

This information management system becomes the means gifted students use to navigate the social expectations and the mixed messages society holds about them. These three beliefs are called the Stigma of Giftedness Paradigm (SGP; Coleman, 1985). The SGP has been studied for years and found to be a good way to understand and explain gifted students' experiences in school settings. Social cognition and coping strategies also can be explained by the SGP.

Recently, some important writings have attempted to compare and contrast the developmental patterns of gifted students by comparing them to patterns of typical development. Some of the more idiosyncratic patterns of development are also being explored. By the latter, I mean the development of gifted students that reflects their own emerging biologically determined qualities, natural developmental tendencies, environmental opportunities, agency, and specific opportunities for development in areas atypical to others. This area of study will require decades of exploration. For now, I think that, in order to understand the lives of gifted students, it is important to note one's time in history, large societal influences, more localized social expectations, and specific patterns of influence on gifted children.

An important finding in an early study was that young gifted students perceive expectations and societal messages through the eyes of an immature mind. Because their social and emotional development often is more age-appropriate than their academic ability, consideration of the early perceptions of mixed messages on their development needs serious ongoing study.

What can we say about gifted students' experiences in school? They receive mixed messages. Some messages are at the macro level, while others are at the micro level. Others are internal to the individual. They try to understand and live within the messages they receive. They develop social-coping strategies to blend in with their environments to the extent they desire. Gifted students experience the same societal influences as their nongifted peers. For example, access to weapons, suicidal patterns, and familial problems or issues (e.g., divorce rates) also impact them. All of these influences also are affected by friendships and idiosyncratic qualities of the individual. For example, an individual's level of mental health is a key ingredient to both his or her experiences in school and his or her behaviors.

All of these influences bring us to the 1999 shootings at Columbine High School in Littleton, CO. Before I comment specifically on that event, I want to add to the equation a few other influences that are important, yet rarely discussed. All students are forced by law to be in the presence of other students for several hours a day in close proximity. Teachers typically have their time dedicated to specific tasks that direct their time and energy to certain settings. What emerge are behaviors from the students that society either allows or does not actively discourage. For example, some adults assume that, in school, students bully each other and girls need to learn how to be able to turn away those who harass them. From a sociological perspective, I assert that a society's prejudices are allowed to exist within schools. Racism, sexism, classism, and so forth are present and active in most schools. The fact that these exist in school is not meant to be a criticism of teachers. I have a great deal of respect for teachers as the individuals who often end or prevent these problems. We can take as an example of the rampant prejudice held by students a group that has for years been subjected to numerous types of assaults: gay and lesbian students. This group illustrates how difficult it is to exist in these microcosms of society we call schools. When the mixed messages that gifted students experience are factored in with the extent to which other prejudices manifest themselves in schools, it is quite amazing to me that gifted kids tend to be as well adjusted as they are.

Several parents of gifted students have told me that their children have surprised them by saying that, while they do not condone the shooting of other students at Columbine, they can understand the feelings of rage that go along with being tormented in school. These parents drew on their own experiences to conclude that trials and tribulations—vis-à-vis bullying and harassment—of students today are the same as those they had as children. Students' experiences in school today are somewhat similar to and somewhat different from the experiences of previous generations. How they are the same is important, and how they are different is very important. Children should feel safe while in school. They cannot thrive when they feel threatened. They grow up knowing anyone who gets mad at them can easily access a gun. Their antagonist may even have the gun with him or her while at school. Even those few people from previous generations who did have similar worries would not have had to seriously consider the possibility of contending with automatic weapons or pipe bombs.

The final factor I believe to be pertinent to the experience of gifted students in school is that the beliefs adults hold about gifted students often are unspoken to them. They only come to realize what they believe when faced with events or circumstances that bring to the surface their actual beliefs or feelings. For example, a few years ago a sophisticated reporter for the *Chicago Tribune* interviewed me about Theodore Kaczynski, the "Unabomber." The reporter had worked for weeks putting together a story about Kaczynski's history that emphasized the fact that he was a gifted student. Several leaders in the field of gifted education were interviewed. The reporter asked me, "Did Ted Kaczynski commit murder because he was allowed to skip two grades in school?" What an amazing assumption! Does accelerating gifted students cause them to become serial killers? My response was, "I hope not, because tens of thousands of students are grade-skipped each year." I was stunned to learn that such an educated person could hold such foolish misconceptions. Imagine what messages people who are not well-educated or academically oriented send to gifted students. Also imagine how gifted students are actually treated if large numbers of adults, including well-educated adults, hold such wild misconceptions about them.

Putting the Pieces Together

Gifted students need adults to guide them. They need adults who understand them to help them develop with few limitations. Although patterns and trends among people can be understood at the macro level, acts of individuals must be understood at the individual level. The students at Columbine who murdered their classmates have been described in the press as gifted students. The lesson of Columbine is not that gifted students are homicidal; rather, it is that the children who killed other students had certain qualities, histories, and experiences. They had access to lethal weapons and the time to plan the killings. Their giftedness should in no way be assumed as a cause agent in their inappropriate act. Their behavior has become a mirror for society's prejudice. A lesson of Columbine should be that schools must create safe environments where learning can thrive. Larger issues like the relationship between the size of schools and the social milieu should be considered. Our research has suggested that being gifted in differing types of school settings leads to different experiences.

Another important question should be, "What size or configuration of school allows for optimal relationships to be forged among students, between students and teachers, and students and guidance counselors?" Few professionals who work in or with public schools believe that we are able to create optimal educational settings. We seem destined to work with what we have. For example, some high schools are so large that their school counselors rarely get to know the students for whom they are responsible. In Indiana, the ratio of high school students to school counselors often exceeds 400 to 1. This speaks to the extent to which schools are not effectively designed to prevent incidents like the one at Columbine. Rather than finding easy, quick condemnations for gifted students, we must commit ourselves to helping all students thrive, including gifted students.

Looking for ways to create positive environments in which all of these students can coexist and actually thrive should be a goal of our society. Blaming schools, television violence, video violence, or divorce rates for the events at Columbine are superficial and will only lead to Band-Aid™ approaches to long-term complicated problems. Although I am troubled about the deaths of the victims at Columbine, I am hoping that Americans will recognize that our culture tolerates the abuse of disempowered students to such a degree that it requires a rare event to bring it to the surface.

FOR DISCUSSION

- Was the Columbine incident a catalyst for change in your school?
- Comment on the question stated in the chapter: What size or configuration of school allows for optimal relationships to be forged among students and guidance counselors?

CHAPTER 25

The Rage of Gifted
Students

KEY CONCEPTS

- Bronfenbrenner's ecological approach to contexts of development
- Gifted students and the influence of macrosystems, exosystems, meso-systems, and microsystems on their lives
- Social milieus in schools and the idiosyncratic patterns of effects on a gifted student's development

The experiences of gifted students in school are quite varied and reflect a wide variety of factors. For 20 years, I have written about their experiences from two perspectives, that of a researcher and that of the students themselves (using their own words). I have come to believe that the lived experiences of gifted students in school are some of the richest areas in the field of gifted education in which to conduct research.

I believe that we are far from understanding the relationship among the experiences of gifted students, how they make sense of these experiences, and how these experiences affect gifted students' behaviors in school and their long-term psychological development. As our society has evolved, our schools increasingly have become a setting where all of society's values interact. Our beliefs, hopes, aspirations, and prejudices coexist in tight physical quarters. Some schools, such as a new $74 million high school in Indiana, provide students with beautiful surroundings and state-of-the-art equipment. Other schools, as so eloquently documented by Jonathan Kozol in his book *Savage Inequalities: Children in America's Schools* (1991), are disgraceful, rundown facilities, struggling to provide their students with such basic necessities as textbooks. Schools exist in the largest cities and the smallest towns. All of them have two things in common—policymakers who rely on them to acculturate students into the preferred mold, and the expectation that this will be done for the least amount of money possible. All children, starting from age 5 or 6, attend school because it is the law. In all of these various settings, parents hope that their children's lives will be improved by earning a good education.

All of these factors and circumstances exist within a large system of dominant beliefs and ideologies that Bronfenbrenner (1994) described as a macrosystem in his ecological approach to contexts of development. The *macrosystem* is the larger context of values and mores that influence the behaviors of students. The next system, the *exosystem*, includes linkages between two or more settings that affect the individual. Mass media, governmental agencies, educational systems, and religious hierarchy may impact the individual indirectly. The *mesosystem* is where the various *microsystems* interact. The individual lives daily in the *microsystem* of his or her school, home, and neighborhood. For example, a gifted adolescent lives with his or her family and attends a local school (microsystem), sees his or her school friends in church or in the neighborhood (mesosystem), and learns from the mass media about stereotypes he or she should hold (exosystem), all within the framework of Christian capitalism, the dominant ideology of our country (macrosystem). The public schools in the United States have been described as anti-intellectual environments (Howley et al., 1995), an attitude promoted in the exosystem, dealt with directly in the mesosystem, and perhaps causing conflict daily in the microsystem.

These various layers of influence on gifted students' experiences cut across their values and cause them to look for meaning in those experiences. Gifted students often receive mixed messages from the ideas and values represented in the exo- and mesosystems. Common mixed messages older gifted students experience include claims by some adults that giftedness does not exist, does not matter, or that gifted students are already advantaged and should not receive any special consideration. Parents encourage them to do well in school, while at the same time, students describe their experiences in school primarily as being bored and waiting for other students to catch up. Perceptions of how they are valued in school, how students and adults treat them, are created and internalized, sometimes leading to feelings of rage. According to *Webster's College Dictionary* (Costello, 1992), one definition for rage is "a violent desire or passion"(p. 1113). Although very few gifted students act out in violent ways, many do seem to acknowledge internalized feelings of rage. This chapter will attempt to articulate what I believe is a deep-seated rage many gifted students feel. I will note how I came to this conclusion and a few ideas about what we might be able to do to improve the situation.

Throughout my career, I have observed, interviewed, counseled, and tested gifted students. To date, I have accumulated data from approximately a dozen states and 15,000 gifted students, mostly from school and program evaluations I have conducted. My professional interest has always been to try to capture the essence of their experiences and to eventually create a model of development representing their stories. I have come to believe that gifted students are affected by their experiences in differing school settings in individual ways. For example, in small rural schools, students describe the experience of being gifted as being part of a family or community. On the other hand, students in large suburban schools describe feelings of being stereotyped with limited social latitude. A function of this experience often is to maintain the social status one has by playing a role—in this case, the stereotypical gifted student. Avoiding threats to the role status becomes a priority, leading students to avoid taking positive risks and to create social-coping strategies. In essence, the social milieu of each school is different, causing idiosyncratic patterns of effects on a student's development.

The media reported several incidents of homicide in high schools in the 1990s. "Reported" is an understatement. The stories were broadcast over and over and over. Perhaps the most dramatic of these tragedies occurred in 1999 at Columbine High School in Littleton, CO. The news portrayed the events hourly for weeks. The lesson we took away from these broadcasts was that our children are not safe in school, and that there is an (implied) additional threat from gifted students. The lesson we should have learned from this tragedy is that our children's experiences in high school (and middle school and elementary school) cause them to suffer. After the events at Columbine, I interviewed dozens of adolescent gifted students about the event. They all stated that what the killers did was wrong and unforgivable, but those I interviewed all knew how they felt. *They knew how the killers felt.* I was quite taken by this. Adults were acting flabbergasted, looking for every conceivable explanation for the murders: video games, access to weaponry, giftedness. I have since gone back and reread samples of transcripts and tape recordings of dozens of interviews I conducted over the past 15 years, and I was dismayed to find that the same thread was often conveyed. Because no tragic events were at the front of the minds of the gifted students being interviewed then, I had phrased my questions in ways that did not encourage this type of evidence to appear as directly as it did in the post-Columbine interviews. But, in one way or another, many of the gifted students provided evidence of feeling rage about the ways they were treated.

One of my former gifted students, who had returned to his alma mater to build a Beowulf system of multiple computers, showed me a website (http://slashdot.org/articles/99/04/25/1438249.shtml) made up of approximately 30 pages of adults' and high school students' comments about their high school experience. Jon Katz (2001) serialized the comments into the "Voices From the Hellmouth" series. Many of the hundreds of contributors nationwide self-reported being gifted students. Their rage is palpable. Below is the quote of one contributor to this serial.

> I stood up in social studies class—the teacher wanted a discussion—and said I could never kill anyone or condone anyone who did kill anyone. But I could, on some level, understand these kids in Colorado, the killers. Because day after day, slight after slight, exclusion after exclusion, you can learn how to hate, and that hatred grows and takes you over sometimes, especially when you come to see that you're hated only because you're smart and different, or sometimes even because you are online a lot, which is still so uncool to many kids. After class, I was called to the principal's office and told that I had to agree to undergo five sessions of counseling or be expelled

from school, as I had expressed sympathy with the killers in Colorado, and the school had to be able to explain itself if I acted out. In other words, for speaking freely, and to cover their ass, I was not only branded a weird geek, but a potential killer. That will sure help deal with violence in America. Jay (Original Comment #1)

How widespread is this problem? Unfortunately I cannot answer this question. I do believe that it exists and to a much greater degree that adults know.

What can we do to help gifted students reduce or eliminate their feelings of rage? How much of this is normal teen angst? Turn of the century psychologist G. Stanley Hall (1904) described adolescence as a period of "storm and stress." His work, along with that of other psychodynamic psychologists, created widespread belief that adolescents necessarily go through such periods. More recent developmental psychologists have largely discredited these claims. Many espouse the belief that some adolescents have this conflict-ridden experience throughout adolescence, while others only experience the conflict episodically. Many do not experience adolescence as a difficult period at all (Offer & Offer, 1975). My contention is that the mixed messages gifted students receive across the various systems that Bronfenbrenner (1994) outlined, along with normal developmental issues, plus the repetitious images of adolescents engaging in homicides, suicides, and other undesirable behavior, all contribute to the rage. Unfortunately, because most adults had some undesirable experiences while in school, they believe that what gifted students experience is just the same rite of passage they endured. Although I have little doubt that some of the current experiences gifted students are having would fit into that category, I contend that contemporary gifted students experience taunting, bullying, and generalized, threatening behavior in different ways than in the past. The media has created the belief in the minds of our students that they are not safe in schools.

The first step toward helping these students is to acknowledge that their experiences are not exactly the same as ours. Another is to work with schools to bring about nonthreatening environments that do not tolerate any taunting or bullying. There also is the need to work toward sending consistent messages to gifted students about their value, worth, and responsibilities. The last suggestion for improvement cuts across most levels of Bronfenbrenner's (1994) model, with families and teachers trying to bring about change locally. Because the greatest influence on gifted students will likely come from the individual and microsystems, beginning there makes the most sense. Disallowing negative remarks and anti-intellectual behavior and encouraging respect for individuals of all ability levels and interests can be done and almost certainly will improve the conditions of all students in school.

FOR DISCUSSION

- How would you respond if someone made the comment that feelings of rage in students is normal teen angst?
- What can families and teachers do to bring about change at the local level to improve conditions for gifted children?

CHAPTER 26

The Many Faces
of Bullies

- Broadening definitions of bullies
- Perceived threats in the lives of gifted students

Gifted students today experience many disruptions in their lives. Some of these disruptions are relatively unique to them, such as needing to hide how well they do in school as a means of fitting into an anti-intellectual school environment (Coleman & Cross, 2001). Other disruptions are believed to be common to many students, such as facing bullies.

We have all seen bullies on television shows, and can even name some of the bullies from our childhood days. We tend to think of bullies (for the most part) as larger than average, dull, mean-spirited males who taunt and physically push around weaker boys during an ongoing, tormented relationship. Ironically, a romantic notion often is maintained about bullies as well—"If he just knew me, he would treat me better" or "All he needs is for one person to stand up to him and he will back down."

Although examples of this stereotypical bully do exist in real life, maintaining this 1950s Hollywood depiction provides a disservice to our gifted students. According to *Webster's Dictionary*, a bully is "a person who hurts, frightens, threatens, or tyrannizes over those who are smaller or weaker." This is a convenient definition supporting the stereotypes propagated in films and television programs. If one focuses more on the outcome of the efforts of the bullies rather than the intentions, a much broader array of people qualify as bullies of gifted students.

Let me provide a slightly different definition of a bully. A bully is a person who uses any approach at his or her disposal including, but not limited to, intimidation (physical, emotional, or verbal), positional authority, relational authority, or societal authority to create limiting effects on another's behaviors, thoughts, or feelings. With this definition, one can easily see how many different people can disrupt their lives. For example, bullies can now be recognized as coming in all sizes, shapes, and from various backgrounds. They are male and female, struggling and successful students, representing all age groups. They are accomplished at being bullies, and are unaware that they are bullies. The faces of bullies are as many as are the behaviors in which they engage to disrupt the lives of others.

My observation is that the operative list of bullies who gifted students actually deal with includes parents and other relatives, teachers, coaches, administrators, counselors, librarians, strangers, and even other gifted students. A few common examples include school administrators' claims that all kids are gifted or that no kids are gifted, and then their denial of reasonable requests to accommodate the student's learning need; a physical education teacher's criticisms of a gifted student's lack of interest in, passion for, or success in athletic endeavors; a classroom teacher's discouragement of questions by gifted students, and the discounting of gifted students' desires to pursue their academic passions. This group of bullies' common bond is the effect of their behavior on the lives of gifted students. More specifically, such bullies disrupt the normal development of gifted students by creating a perceived threat in the mind of the gifted student. In its purest form, to bully is to control others.

How does this play out in the lives of gifted students? Before I address this, let us remember that our children are growing up during a time when they perceive threats all around them. My generation was raised to fear nuclear war and the Red Menace. Occasional drills were held to "protect students from nuclear attack." Although the drills provided an occasional reminder that some adults were worried, the technology to create and support a high level of chronic worry in children did not exist then as it does today. Today, there are more than 200 television channels, multiple competing news outlets, the Internet, and newspapers that constantly bombard children with images of threats to their survival.

As I grew older, the threat of nuclear war faded. Today's youth receive messages 24 hours a day telling them that their schools are not safe, their homes are not safe, their communities are not safe, and, on the horizon, there are numerous countries led by crazed anti-American dictators determined to end life as we know it. Added to this mix are additional messages that gifted students receive that they are deviating from the norm (Coleman & Cross, 1988). It is within this context that our gifted students understand bullies. Local circumstances that may reveal actual physical threats to their well-being also must be considered. For example, youths in certain settings may live among gun-wielding gangs, but many do not. In essence, this phenomenon combines real and merely perceived threats to both one's physical and social safety at a time in history when media outlets suggest that no one is safe.

I would like to point out one more factor in this mixture: the effectiveness of variable reinforcement schedules on human behavior. Against the gray backdrop of violence, all it takes for people to affirm their fears of threats against their safety are occasional acts of violence. The violence can even be half a world away and still reinforce these perceptions. Given this historical context in which gifted students live, how can we help guide their social and emotional development as it pertains to dealing with bullies? Here are a few ways:

◈ Learn a broader definition of bullying behavior.
◈ Realize that bullying behavior can be both intentional and unintentional.
◈ Learn to recognize the different ways in which one can be bullied.
◈ Learn strategies for dealing with others' bullying behaviors.
◈ Test perceptions—gifted students need to learn how to approach the perceived bully about the person's actual intentions. This is especially true when dealing with teachers and other school personnel.

❖ Use sounding boards—gifted students need to use others as sounding boards to help them test their perceptions.

❖ Use self-talk—gifted students need to engage in self-talk about what the actual intention of the bullying behavior is.

❖ Use counseling—gifted students need to create a fluid counseling relationship that can provide support and problem-solving opportunities for the student. It also can help by enlisting an adult as an advocate.

Armed with these skills, gifted students can reduce impediments and disruptions to their positive development. As the primary caretakers of students with gifts and talents, let us join forces to help these students reach their potential as people.

FOR DISCUSSION

- What is your definition of a bully?

- As a teacher, parent, or counselor, what steps can you take to reduce perceived threats for gifted children?

- As a teacher, parent, or counselor, discuss strategies that may be effective in dealing with bullying behaviors.

CHAPTER 27

Psychological Autopsy Provides Insight Into Gifted Adolescent Suicide

- Psychological autopsy
- Commonalities and themes that emerged from study

In the chapter "Examining Claims About Gifted Children and Suicide," I mentioned a study conducted on the suicides of three gifted adolescents. That study appeared in a special issue of *The Journal of Secondary Gifted Education* (Cross, Cook, & Dixon, 1996). This chapter will highlight the findings of the study entitled "Psychological Autopsies of Three Academically Talented Adolescents Who Committed Suicide." I hope this information will assist others in the identification of gifted students who are at risk for suicidal behavior so that intervention can take place.

Background Information

The three adolescent males in this study had attended a state-funded, residential high school for 300 academically talented 11th- and 12th-grade students in a Midwestern state.

Research Methods

The psychological autopsy was designed to assess a variety of factors, including behaviors, thoughts, feelings, and relationships of an individual who is deceased (Ebert, 1987). It was originally developed as a means of resolving equivocal deaths and has expanded to include the analysis of nonequivocal suicides, with the intention of reducing their likelihood in similar groups of people (Jones, 1977; Neill, Benensohn, Farber, & Resnick, 1974). It can be used as a posthumous evaluation of mental, social, and environmental influences on the suicide victim. The psychological autopsy includes information from two areas: interviews with people who had significant relationships with the victim (e.g., parents, siblings, friends, teachers, romantic partners) and archival information related to the victim (e.g., school records, test information, medical records, personal letters, essays, diaries, suicide notes, artwork). Investigators analyze the information to identify themes and issues that may be valuable in the prediction of suicide within similar groups of people.

Results

The results have been organized into three categories: commonalities with adolescent suicide, commonalities among the three cases related to their giftedness, and themes that emerged across the three cases. The results have been excerpted with permission from the article "Psychological Autopsies of Three Academically Talented Adolescents Who Committed Suicide" by Cross, Cook, and Dixon (1996).

Commonalities With Adolescent Suicide in the General Population

1. All subjects were adolescent Caucasian males.
2. They each manifested four emotional commonalities:
   ◇ depression,
   ◇ anger,

◇ mood swings, and

◇ confusion about the future.

3. They each manifested three behavioral commonalities:
   ◇ poor impulse control,
   ◇ substance use and abuse, and
   ◇ extensive journaling.

4. They each manifested four relational commonalities:
   ◇ romantic relationship difficulties,
   ◇ self-esteem difficulties (either by exaggeration or by self-condemnation),
   ◇ conflicted family relationships, and
   ◇ isolation from persons capable of disconfirming irrational logic.

5. The subjects shared warning signs in six categories:
   ◇ behavior problems;
   ◇ period of escalation of problems;
   ◇ constriction (withdrawal, friends, dichotomous thinking, talk of suicide);
   ◇ talk about suicide;
   ◇ changes in school performance; and
   ◇ family histories of psychological problems.

Commonalities Among the Three Cases Related to Their Giftedness

1. The subjects exhibited overexcitabilities:
   ◇ expressed in ways or levels beyond the norm even among their gifted peers;
   ◇ had minimal prosocial outlets;
   ◇ experienced difficulty separating fact from fiction, especially regarding overidentification with negative asocial or aggressive characters or themes in books and movies;
   ◇ experienced intense emotions;

◇ felt conflicted, pained, and confused; and

◇ devalued emotional experience, except for pain.

2. They each expressed polarized, hierarchical, egocentric value systems.

3. They each engaged in group discussions of suicide as a viable and honorable solution.

4. They each expressed behavior consistent with Dabrowski's Level II or Level III of Positive Disintegration.

5. They each attended residential school as a means of escape (e.g., from family, hometown).

Themes Emerging Across the Three Cases

1. All three suffered from depression. Case 1 was hospitalized for depression; Case 2 was a classic marked depressive (his journal clearly reflects the depressive thoughts of negative view of self and negative view of the future); and Case 3 was identified as in need of treatment by school personnel, and his journal reflects clinical depression.

2. Suicide contagion seemed to have been operative: Case 3 seemed to particularly follow Case 2, while Case 1 set the stage for the discussion of suicide. The suicide of the musical group Nirvana's lead singer, Kurt Cobain, also was related.

3. Suicide has a cultural component: music (e.g., Nirvana, Jane's Addiction, Sex Pistols), literature (e.g., Anne Rice, H. P. Lovecraft), and movies (e.g., *Heathers*) all played important parts for these adolescents. Even though many teenagers may consume similar media, among these three there seemed to be an excessive focus on dark, negative content.

4. They had many characteristics identified as overexcitabilities (e.g., very sensitive, two were vegetarians, fantasy, mixing truth and fiction).

5. Suicide has a social component. The topic of suicide was openly discussed among the students in their peer groups; their discussions reduced the taboo associated with suicide and supported

the position that suicide was a free choice that was their decision to make. As a result, there was no need to seek help or make referrals.

6. Excessive introspection and obsessive thinking was evident. The journals served as ways to avoid interaction with others, and, as a result, irrational thinking fed itself rather than being disconfirmed by others.

7. The issue of control over others was present in two cases. This control resulted in attempts to harm another in one case.

Unanswered Questions

The following is a list of questions that remained largely unanswered at the end of the study.

1. How large a role does suicide contagion play in multiple suicides?

2. What role does unsupervised journaling play in suicide?

3. What is the extent of influence that overexcitabilities play in suicide ideation and behavior?

4. Does exploring dark issues by this age group make its members vulnerable to suicide?

5. What is the effect on suicide behavior of residential schools aggregating students with similar high-risk factors (e.g., previous suicide ideation or attempts) in a setting that encourages self-exploration?

6. What role does the combination of asynchronous development and dark literature play in suicide ideation?

7. What role does the lack of religious beliefs have on suicide behavior?

8. What is the influence of popular cultural icons who commit suicide on suicide behavior of gifted adolescents?

9. What effect does believing suicide is an honorable option have on suicide behavior?

10. What is the role that popular media, where violence (including suicide and homicide) is pervasive, have on suicide behavior?

I offer these suggestions for you to consider as you think about the social and emotional needs of gifted children. You are cautioned to remember that the results were based on only three cases and therefore may not be representative of the larger phenomenon.

Recommendations for Preventing the Suicides of Gifted Adolescents

1. Keep an eye out for the following:
   ◇ emotional difficulties, especially anger or depression;
   ◇ lack of prosocial activities;
   ◇ dissatisfaction with place, situation, school, peers, family, or self;
   ◇ difficulties in romantic relationships, especially with peers of similar abilities;
   ◇ non-normative expression of overexcitabilities, especially unbalanced expression of overexcitabilities (predominantly negative, asocial, or antisocial); and
   ◇ difficulty separating fact from fiction (overidentification with characters, especially antiheroes and aggressive characters).

2. Err on the side of caution.
   ◇ Do not overlook potential signs of suicide just because the child is gifted.
   ◇ Accept the uniqueness of gifted adolescents, but not at the risk of overlooking indicators of emotional, psychological, or suicidal distress.

3. Be proactive.
   ◇ Educate gifted adolescents about their emotional experiences and needs.
   ◇ Communicate, communicate, communicate.
   ◇ Challenge the idea that suicide is an honorable solution.

◇ Strive for a balance of positive and negative themes and characters in curricula, books, and audiovisual materials.

◇ Assess for emotional, psychological, and relational difficulties.

◇ When in doubt, do something!

FOR DISCUSSION

- Discuss the strengths and limitations to using the psychological autopsy as a research method.

- The study resulted in a large number of unanswered questions. Select one of these questions and comment on it in relation to gifted individuals.

- Investigate what systems or procedures exist in your school/community to deal with students who exhibit warning signs of potential suicide.

SECTION 4

Where We Have Been and Where We Are Going

This section of the book starts off with two special commentary pieces, "Don't Forget the Little Guys," by Nancy Robinson, and "Three Questions" by Maureen Neihart. Both address the potential future of the field of gifted education and the differences present among even a narrow population of students.

In the first chapter, "Contemporary Issues in the Psychosocial Development of Students With Gifts and Talents," I examine some of the contemporary issues that have affected gifted students most significantly, including the events of September 11, 2001 and the No Child Left Behind Act. The following chapter continues this contemporary theme and begins to look forward as I discuss "The Changing Life Metaphor of Gifted Youth."

In the chapter that follows, the work of Margaret Mead, anthropologist extraordinaire, provides a foundation for a further look into our "Changing Times." Anthropological studies of cultural change reveal the complexity of our current state. We are all pioneers, the youth among us even more than the adults. As we work to help gifted students find their way, we must learn about the influences unique to our time.

The next chapter, "Top Ten (Plus or Minus Two) List for the 20th Century," was not one of my regular columns. For *Gifted Child Today*'s end-of-the-millennium issue, several professionals in the field of gifted education were asked to overview what they believed were the most important events that occurred during the past century, with an eye on predicting the future of the field. The ideas conveyed represent my way of thinking, which tends to emphasize connections while trying to understand historical patterns. I also tend to believe that sociopolitical forces influence many of the important trends in educational policy and practice.

Continuing the examination of education practices, the final chapter discusses the idea of educational equality in the context of Kurt Vonnegut's short story "Harrison Bergeron," in which a Handicapper General makes all citizens equal. This chapter, "Disrupting Social Contracts That Affect Gifted Students: An Homage to 'Harrison Bergeron'" also addresses the idea of social contract theory. In combination, the chapters in this section aim to ask readers to look at where the field of gifted education is currently in regard to children's social and emotional lives, and where it could be in years to come.

Don't Forget the Little Guys

by Nancy Robinson

One of the consequences of the fact that educators are by far the majority of those concerned with giftedness is that school-age children have commanded the lion's share of research attention. They are, of course, a population of convenience as well as a responsibility that teachers do (and should) take seriously, but few educators of gifted students have turned their attention to younger children or adults. It is psychologists, by and large, who have done so, beginning with Galton and Terman, and, more recently, others such as the Gottfrieds, Simonton, Fagan, Benbow, and Lubinski, just to name a few. I've done my share of work with adolescents enrolled in the Early Entrance Program at the University of Washington, but my heart has always been with the little ones—toddlers and preschoolers—for a number of reasons.

First, of course, all of us are aware that well before children enter school, individual differences are present, sometimes dramatically so. A few behaviors, such as alertness and rapidity of habituation, seem to be indicators during infancy of later advancement, but somewhat more stable individual differences emerge during the second year of life. (Often these indicators are correlated with background variables such as parent education, especially in middle-class families, but the correlations are far from perfect.) Parents often are good at recognizing that their children's development is more rapid than expected in one or more domains, especially in those where age benchmarks are well-known, such as talking and reading. When parent descriptions are merged with objective assessments such as test scores, our longitudinal studies have shown that there can be considerable stability in developmental patterns. The potential certainly is there for early identification and intervention.

There are at least two major reasons why this state of affairs is important. Most compelling is the possibility of discovering and supporting very young children who are living in nonpropitious circumstances and whose development is discernibly ahead of what one would expect. It is these children who are least likely to experience in their families the developmental challenges, focused conversations, outings, book reading, question asking and answering, and parental encouragement that nourish cognitive growth and awaken the curiosity and mastery that carry children forward. Our first task is to train their caretakers—parents and Head Start teachers, for example, as well as formal and informal providers of daycare—to spot those who are ahead and refer them to the services we will hopefully make ready to provide. Training physicians and nurses also is essential. Unfortunately, the most popular assessment device used by pediatricians—the Ages and Stages Questionnaire (ASQ)—alerts attention only when children fail to attain a score at an age-determined cut-off. There is no provision for going beyond the typical. Pediatricians may not be oblivious to a child's advancement, but there is no incentive for them to do anything about it.

One of my studies with math-precocious young children, who were enrolled as they were completing preschool or kindergarten, showed that even minimal early intervention can be effective. A maximum of 28 half-day sessions over a period of 2 years led to significantly greater math advancement in a group given this experience, than in an equally precocious comparison group. Their parents were accurate in identifying and describing their talents, and indeed, even the comparison group stayed distinctly ahead of peers in math reasoning over the 2-year period. It was disappointing to us, however, that despite our visiting Head Start programs to invite teachers to nominate promising students, we were aware of very few Head Start referrals among the nearly 700 parents we heard from. Alerting early-childhood caregivers is unlikely to be an easy task.

Having found these children, of course, the real work begins: working with their parents and caretakers about the importance of their interactions with the children—verbal and otherwise—providing first-class, stimulating preschool experiences; and permitting them the company of other bright children, as well as older children, for part of the day. They should hit the ground running when they enter kindergarten. While we're at it, we need to encourage public schools both to begin providing advanced instruction to all children who enter kindergarten developmentally advanced over their age peers and to abolish the tyranny of the calendar in deciding who is and who isn't ready for school. And we need to provide extended-day and summer programs, as well as parent-school partnerships, to promote the optimal development of children who might otherwise be marginalized and lose their momentum.

Many developmental psychologists do focus on young children, and partnering with them also can have enormous payoffs for us. Studies of gifted children are notoriously poorly funded, with the result that our samples are small and often highly selected. Developmental psychologists often are bothered by the very outliers we love, those who learn the task too fast, talk too much, and otherwise provide "noise" in the data. (The smaller the variance in a sample, the easier it is to find significant differences when groups are compared, so outliers are a nuisance.) Yet these investigators often have big grants, big databases, and statistical analysts on their staffs who with a few computer strokes can deliver us precious information, get another publication for the investigator, and make everyone happy.

Finally, research with precocious young children can help answer a question for which we only act as though we have the expertise to address. The unanswered question has to do with differences—if any— between the mental processing of gifted youngsters and that of their typically developing *mental age* peers. This is a very basic question in considering whether academic acceleration, which is clearly effective, is enough or whether further modifications are needed in students' academic experience. Are these children thinking in more abstract modes than even their mental age peers? Are they more intuitive or global in their thinking? Quicker to make connections?

The development of young children is so rapid that, over a relatively brief span of years, they provide a special window into their individual differences and their possibly unique patterns of growth. There was a flurry of such research in the 1970s and 1980s (and more recently, a mini-flurry by neo-Piagetians) suggesting that gifted children traverse Piagetian stages earlier than other children do, but not as early as we might have expected from their IQs. Having made the conceptual leap, however, they "own it" and generalize rapidly. Approaching the question differently, one of my husband's graduate students, the late Steven McClelland, some 30 years ago compared the successes of younger gifted and older typically developing children with mean mental ages of about 5 years on Stanford-Binet L-M, showing that the gifted children displayed more abstract thinking while their mental age peers succeeded more with hands-on, concrete problems. All these results fit with those of Lannie Kanevsky, who studied typically developing chronological age and mental age peers of gifted children given the Tower of Hanoi problem. But the limited scopes of these investigations need more detail and more tracking over time.

Our work is cut out for us but essentially points toward building partnerships with others outside our field. Some of these people, particularly the physicians and psychologists, were probably gifted children themselves. The task shouldn't be too hard.

Three Questions

by Maureen Neihart

Three questions regarding the social and emotional development of gifted children continue to capture my attention and keep me thinking. The first is, *Are there true qualitative differences?* We know that growing up gifted is a significantly different experience. Gifted children manifest patterns of characteristics that are predictable. But to what extent are these characteristics just the result of advanced cognitive development and to what extent are they real qualitative differences? If we compared a large group of high IQ children to a large group of average IQ children who are 2–3 years older, would we find that the two groups are more similar or more different? I think they would differ more than they're alike but this is research that is yet to be undertaken, so we lack the data to verify the hypothesis.

Some aspects of gifted children's development are probably just a manifestation of their advanced cognitive abilities. For example, their moral reasoning abilities, their unusually good conceptual skills, and their interest and concern in issues of morality, spirituality, and justice may be more a reflection of their cognitive abilities than any true qualitative differences. Even their expectations for friendships, which we also believe are developmentally advanced in gifted children, may have more to do with their accelerated development than with anything else. But I think there are some characteristics that are more qualitative in nature and wouldn't be observed at similar rates in older, average ability children.

For instance, I wouldn't expect intensity (or drive), to correlate with age. Similarly, I think we would also find that perfectionism, sensitivity, and introversion are characteristics that correlate significantly more with IQ than with age. There is some evidence to support this in introversion already. A handful of studies have found that introversion is more common among gifted children. The rate of introversion is about 25% in the general population, but double that among gifted children. However, there are no systematic studies with large sample sizes. This is work that I think is badly needed.

I suspect that were we to compare high IQ children with older, average-ability children, we'd find that the two groups are similar in their moral reasoning abilities, conceptual skills, and in their concerns about moral and spiritual issues, but markedly different in their perfectionism, sensitivity, and introversion. I think it's also likely that the two groups would differ significantly in their academic self-concepts, with the gifted group having more positive academic self-concepts.

Another question that intrigues me is one I've thought about a great deal about since moving to Singapore: *In what ways does culture define giftedness and influence the social and emotional development of gifted children?* Collectivist societies generally, and Chinese societies in particular, hold very different beliefs about ability and talent development, and these beliefs naturally shape the experience of growing up gifted in these cultures. Let me give you an example to illustrate.

When I first moved into my local neighborhood, exam results had recently come out. Singaporean children take a high-stakes national exam at the end of sixth grade, the results of which determine their future educational placement and much of their educational programming over the next 4 years. In my neighborhood, larger-than-life photos of high-scoring children were advertised on banners stretched high across streets and on large placards posted on our neighborhood walls and fences. They were celebrities! All of their test scores were proudly listed next to their photos, along with the names of the elite secondary schools they had been admitted to.

There are profound differences in how Eastern and Western societies think about ability. In the West, ability is believed to be largely due to genetics, with environment playing a supporting role. As a result, parents and teachers generally perceive their role to be one of identifying innate aptitudes and developing them. However, in Eastern societies, people tend to believe that children are born with unlimited potential and that environmental influences are the predominant force in shaping ability. Asians believe that while *rates* of development differ, human potential is actually similar across most children. The implication of this is obvious: With hard work, anything is possible! As a result, definition, identification, and development of talent are approached differently in Asia, by both parents and teachers. There is no formal emphasis on early identification because people believe that time is needed to develop the child's potential giftedness. Hard work is introduced very early and adults expect young children to tolerate and manage much more distress than Western adults do. Competition and comparative rankings are introduced across most domains as soon as a child begins learning. There are exams and "grades" in ballet, music lessons, athletics, and academics, even for private lessons. Also, tracking has been the norm throughout Asia for centuries. Asian countries differ in the age at which tracking begins and in how many levels are offered, but fixed-ability grouping, special classes, and elite schools have an ancient history and are unquestioned. Equity, until only very recently, has been primarily a Western concern. Studying giftedness in Asian contexts has prompted me to examine some of my own assumptions about gifted children and has made me aware of blind spots in my understanding. It has also greatly improved my understanding of the role culture plays in conceptions of human development. I have much to learn!

There is one last question that still nags at me off and on: *Is there a gifted personality?* Personality refers to our persistent pattern of responding to the world around us. The more we learn about personality and the more we learn about gifted people, the more I think there is a gifted personality, but it has been difficult to demonstrate empirically so far. However, I'm aware of several people around the world who are chipping away at this.

We know that there is a creative personality. The research suggests that there are domain-specific differences in the creative personality and certain psychological strengths and vulnerabilities associated with high creativity in different domains. Based on what I understand so far, it seems logical to me that there would be a gifted personality, perhaps also with domain-specific, subtle differences, but we are still a long way from having the kind of data that exists and supports the idea of a creative personality. Perhaps I will get to see this verified or ruled out in my lifetime.

CHAPTER 28

Contemporary Issues in the Psychosocial Development of Students With Gifts and Talents

KEY CONCEPTS

- The effects of 9/11 on psychosocial development
- The impact of No Child Left Behind
- Anti-intellectualism
- "Good" college angst
- Internet and information availability

As adults committed to improving the lives of students, we sometimes come to believe that our children's lives are very much like our own. In some cases I agree. However, increasingly, I have come to see evidence of lived experiences of today's youth that are different than those of prior generations. The accumulation of these differences, affected by historical events, economic swings, new diseases, medical discoveries, political leaders, and so on, leads to an aggregate experience that can be quite different from the previous generation's. To work effectively with students with gifts and talents, we must be active in our pursuit of knowledge about these differences. In this chapter, I will review a series of issues that are quite contemporary and somewhat unique to the lives of students with gifts and talents. In essence, I will be covering five issues that run the gamut from being international and historical to those things that are very specific to the individual person.

The first issue I want to mention is of a historical nature that is both international and national: the world since 9/11. Since 9/11, many things have changed in the United States and the world, and several of them affect the lives of our students with gifts and talents. For example, over the last several years, our young gifted children have led their lives against the backdrop of ongoing war. They have heard about war on a daily basis; they have seen images of terrorism and bombings, and they have come face to face with images of Americans being tortured and engaging in torture. These topics were not in their consciousness just a few years ago. Over the past several years, our gifted children have been living their lives with all of these negative events directly in their visual field and yet a world apart; ever-present in their consciousness, but not so in their daily life activities. They have learned that the ideals on which their country was founded were quickly sacrificed under the banner of security. In my opinion, these issues in combination have created considerable anxiety for many of them. Although people vary in how they are affected by these issues, they are affected. In general, my belief is that this generation or cohort of gifted children is living their lives with heightened anxiety. All aspects of a person's life are affected when they live in an anxious state. Parents, teachers, and counselors must be vigilant in monitoring the anxiety levels of students so appropriate counseling can be made available to them.

The second contemporary issue that has had a major effect on psychosocial development of students with gifts and talents is the national No Child Left Behind (NCLB; 2001) policy, a part of the Elementary and Secondary Education Act. NCLB was created with some good intentions. Unfortunately, however, it was not funded properly and has some important unintended by-products. For example, with its emphasis on annual yearly progress (AYP), a punitive model was created wherein schools have been compelled to focus their time and energy on a narrow band of students who have the capacity to pass a minimum competency exam in their state. The long-term effect on children with gifts and talents has been little to no money or encouragement for schools to provide a rigorous education for them. Many educators have complained vociferously that students with gifts and talents have been neglected educationally since NCLB became federal policy.

To the detriment of all children with gifts and talents, it is clear that they are living their lives in a country that is largely anti-intellectual. Although there are exceptions, in general it is a fair statement to say that the United States does not value exceptional intellect. Schools exhibit this mindset, many families do, and the general population does as well. Consequently, research has demonstrated for decades that, if you are an intellectually inclined gifted student, you must find ways to cope with the anti-intellectual nature of our schools (Coleman & Cross, 1988). These coping behaviors often are time-wasters and possibly are damaging to the student's development. The gifted students conclude that they cannot be their true selves while in school, that they have to hide or mask part of themselves, and that who they actually are as people is not acceptable to others in school (Cross et al., 1991). Considerable research over the years has illustrated and revealed the kinds of social coping behaviors that gifted kids will often engage in from living their lives in this anti-intellectual environment. This sentiment is especially prominent in media in commercials and certain types of television shows such as situation comedies. Anti-intellectual environments are not conducive to the psychological well-being of students with gifts and talents, nor are they conducive to their reaching their fullest potential.

Particularly pervasive among children with gifts and talents are the pressures associated with going to college. This particular subset of our population—our students with gifts and talents—often feels considerable pressure to make virtually perfect grades, score as high as possible on the SAT and the ACT, and get admitted into a very small number of specific colleges and universities. Having worked with secondary-aged gifted students for many years, I have come to believe that because so many of our children start life with very little support in backgrounds of financial poverty, a large portion of our gifted population really cannot be competitive enough, either on tests or in the admissions process, to be admitted into top tier colleges and universities. The students feel the pressure and you see it manifest in all sorts of stress-related activities, from cutting behavior, to drinking, to underachievement. It takes a terrible toll on this group of children whose positive development we are trying to support.

Access to the Internet is another contemporary issue in the psychosocial development of children with gifts and talents. The Internet will likely be proven by history to be one of the few truly significant changes that had worldwide effects—probably on par with the printing press, perhaps greater. The Internet provides access to information and images that just a few years ago we could not even imagine possible. It also encourages a type of learning that is very engaged. It is child-centered learning. Children feel considerable control when they are involved with the Internet. Of course, the other side of these issues is that the Internet puts them at risk for interacting with predators. It gives them access to information and materials that may not be developmentally appropriate, if at all appropriate. It can become a time-sink in that they may spend all or most of their time engaging in only the activities that are of interest to them. It may encourage considerable breadth of knowledge but very little depth. At one time it was acknowledged that children had a school curriculum and a rival curriculum that included things like television and social activities. Now that metaphor is probably incomplete, because it appears that the Internet provides an access and type of learning that requires a different kind of engagement than traditional ways of learning. In fact, the student-centered nature of the learning that takes place using the Internet may transcend the formal school curriculum. That fact is putting the student in a very different situation from students in earlier generations, as formal instruction in school often is quite teacher-directed. Some argue that, for the first time in the history of the United States, our children are more advanced in the use of technology than the teachers who teach them. That fact brings to bear all sorts of ramifications. In some ways the Internet is allowing for friendships to be made around passion areas, such as interests in art or music, and it provides a tool for gifted kids who are more introverted to meet people. There are many legitimate and positive ways in which the Internet is changing lives. It also is redefining our culture in terms of rules of communication, power relationships, and the development of expertise that may prove to be very beneficial over time, but right now are somewhat unsettling, especially for the older generation. How it affects today's youth remains to be seen.

In summary, these five issues strike me as being particularly salient in the psychosocial development of students with gifts and talents today. Although I do not have answers to many of the questions I posed that pertain to these areas, I think it is very important that we continue to do research and try to help our children with these matters so they can develop in a very healthy way and hopefully maximize their potential. Researchers need to explore how these contemporary issues have changed and are changing the lives of our students with gifts and talents so we can more effectively guide them.

FOR DISCUSSION

- What other major changes in society or environment do you think have affected students with gifts and talents?

- Do you think these changes have been positive or negative for young people?

CHAPTER 29

The Changing Life Metaphor of Gifted Youth

KEY CONCEPTS

- The shaping power of metaphor
- Dominant metaphors in society
- Identity formation

Metaphors influence our perceptions and thinking, from fairly inconsequential concepts, to some of the most basic matters. A root metaphor is one that is foundational to other beliefs and conceptions. These root metaphors become a primary mechanism we employ to understand our world. We see evidence in the metaphors we use of our underlying beliefs, and evidence in our behavior of the metaphors underpinning our beliefs. Metaphors not only represent our understanding, they also act to shape our understanding. There seems to be a major change in the metaphor currently underpinning our society. In this chapter, I explore what I believe has become the dominant root metaphor of today's gifted youth. I illustrate some of the antecedents of the change and some of the outcomes of the current metaphor being employed.

According to Lakoff and Johnson (1980), metaphors are foundational to our understanding of our world because they "structure how we perceive, how we think, and what we do" (p. 4). Rather than merely being linguistic creations as originally thought, metaphors actually represent the inner workings of the mind. Cognitive psychologists such as George Lakoff study language and analyze metaphors as a means to more fully understand the thought patterns of individuals.

Metaphors contain a topic and vehicle that are linked by a common ground (Winner, 1988). A topic becomes better understood by applying attributes or characteristics of the vehicle to it. For example, the saying that "Time is money" suggests that time has features of value, is a commodity, and can be used up. How we perceive and experience time becomes affected by the characteristics of money. Our society has representative sayings that support this claim. "Wasting time," "spending time," and "borrowed time" are examples for this metaphor that Lakoff and Johnson (1980) have written about. We also understand such important concepts as *success*, *good*, and *smart* metaphorically.

Antecedents to the Change in Root Metaphor

It is my contention that the evolution of an emerging metaphor of *life as entertainment* has been influenced by several factors. The most obvious is the hyper-changing nature of the technology available to children. With the realization of so many forms of technology using digital architecture, an amalgamation across discrete technologies is occurring that allows for users to have significantly different experiences. From these changes, communications across groups is possible in real time and among numerous people at one time. The change in communication patterns is changing the nature of our gifted children's lived experiences of relationships.

A second aspect of this change in communication patterns is revealed in the breadth of interactions among children who do not know each other and who cluster around areas of interest. Age ranges vary more than has been typical in the past, and relationship boundaries are being redrawn by the children.

Another characteristic of these changes is in the area of music collection and creation. Children now have access to virtually every song ever recorded and can locate and download the music within minutes of logging onto a computer. Music libraries are growing to incredible levels, with considerable personalization determining what music the child possesses.

The use of new technologies to create music is flourishing in a manner that is remarkable to see. Students who in the past would never have attempted to create their own music are now doing so without ever leaving their computers. It is conceivable that someday all young people will have experienced composing music electronically.

Confluence of Antecedents

With the digitization of the various technologies available to our youth, in just a few short years they have integrated these technologies into their daily routines. They can pursue their interests by using their laptops, smartphones, e-mail, instant messaging, chat rooms, and so forth. Some engage in all of these activities while listening to music, taking pictures, and sending e-mail by using smartphone devices. They communicate, search for information, and create new music on a whim. They can download images on every conceivable topic and create personal museums of art. All of this can be carried out and printed wirelessly. The world is not only their oyster, it is their personalized oyster. The culture of me (note the metaphor) is being taken to new limits, shedding many of the longstanding accoutrements to the psychosocial development of children.

Cultural Influences

In the second half of the 20th century, I believe the most recognizable face in America shifted from that of a scientist (Albert Einstein) to that of a professional athlete (Michael Jordan). This shift represents a change in interests and priorities that effectively taught our children to aspire to athletics and away from an academic focus. The metaphor of success as measured by contributions in the academic arena changed to success as measured by athletic performance. An important difference in these two metaphors is the fact that aspirations of academic work are inherently conducted out of the limelight, while athletic performance is performed primarily as a form of entertainment for the masses. A second important difference between these metaphors is that the primary assumption about the success of the academic is that it depends on hard work and general intelligence. The athletic metaphor is based more on an assumption of innate ability—a natural talent.

With more than 300 television channels available, children's attention has been curried for years. Sports, cartoons, and commercials absorb considerable attention of many of our children. By adding computer time, including all of its advertisers' efforts, one can predict certain outcomes. For example, a few years ago, LeBron James reportedly signed a contract to be paid $94,000,000 to advertise tennis shoes. This was in addition to his extremely large salary to play basketball for the Cleveland Cavaliers. He was 18 years old at the time.

For 2 years, I worked with impoverished children in Louisiana in an 8-week-long summer program held on the campus of a university best known for its engineering degrees. The program brought more than 100 children together who had failed the eighth grade one or more times. They worked half a day, learning employment skills, and were paid minimum wage. The second half of the day was spent with academic instruction in mathematics and language arts. Many of these children became the breadwinners of their families upon receiving their first check. I got to know these children quite well. I had access to their school records, so I studied them and their lives very closely. I played basketball with them, oversaw an extensive counseling program, and generally lived with them for 2 months. They changed my life and helped form many of the beliefs I hold today about our field.

The first important lesson they taught me was that success in school was not solely contingent on academic ability. Their measures of ability revealed a nearly perfect normal distribution, with more than half showing average or greater intellectual abilities and some showing that they needed services for intellectually gifted students. Another lesson I learned through daily experience was that poor minority children are always watched, ridiculed, suspected of being delinquent, and regularly accused of breaking rules. They certainly were not considered able students by many of the adults who worked on the university's campus. For example, I came across a group of the students being lined up against a wall by a university policeman who was accusing them of vandalism. He pointed to marks on a sidewalk. I recognized the chalk outline of the body of Rapunzel. The 30-foot long outline of her hair was a dead giveaway. The artwork was in support of a creative writing class. It was very creative and quite artistic. The level of aggression of the police officer and the message conveyed was very disconcerting to me. The kids attempted to comfort me once I had sent the officer on his way.

They came from abject poverty, but did not complain, feel entitled, or ask for preferential treatment. The teachers in the program were among the best I have been around in 25 years in higher education. The students' academic gains were tremendous. Statistics from the program indicated that those who participated in this program were seven times more likely than comparison groups to graduate from high school.

What is the tie-in to the metaphor emphasis of this chapter? My colleague and I discovered that none of the students could name more than these four occupations: teacher, minister, police officer, and professional athlete. A teacher was a White female (three quarters of the students were male and many were African American), and a person who most of these children had not had good experiences with. Being a minister required a "calling," and they were open to it, but did not aspire to it. A police officer was seen as an enemy, certainly not a profession to pursue. That left professional athlete as their only possible future occupation. Virtually every student attending this program had all of his aspirations focused on becoming a professional athlete, mostly a professional basketball player. Having played ball with them on a daily basis, I learned that most of them had never participated on a formal basketball team. Moreover, their range of athleticism was normally distributed. In essence, the chance of being born into families of abject poverty had doomed them to a cultural ignorance with no reasonable aspirations for the future. The enormous wealth and admiration of a few world-class athletes became their hope for the future. More perniciously, it defined for them a future that could not be had. Imagine being a student in a culture that defines you as a criminal and your only hope is being discovered as a great talent.

The metaphor of success for these young people was clearly entertainment-based. The children of poverty are not the only ones who see the world in this way. Cultural influences have encouraged a metaphorical shifting among most young people today.

Psychosocial Development

Erik Erikson and other psychologists have claimed that children go through predictable developmentally oriented psychosocial crises as they mature. During these periods, common issues are experienced. For example, as children move into early adolescence, they often feel like they are on stage, being watched by others. This feeling can be very strong, causing considerable concern to the young person. Other experiences of self-consciousness are exacerbated by feelings of differentness and inadequacy often felt during puberty. According to Erikson (1963), between the ages of 12 and 16 years, children try to resolve psychosocial crises associated with identity formation. During this time, children grapple with the tension between the need to feel accepted and the desire for attention. They also are contending with issues of fitting in and standing out. These related issues, including feeling on stage, feeling different, desiring attention and wanting to fit in, and being accepted but feeling unique, are important aspects of the lived experiences of our young people.

A related experience of feeling on stage is an anticipation of being discovered. This phenomenon has been elevated to mythical status by tales of the occasional Hollywood actress who was "discovered" while sitting in a local soda shop or at the mall. In the early days of this expectation, the implication was that one would be discovered on the way to becoming both competent and famous. Interestingly, modern-day versions of this phenomenon hold little to no expectation for becoming competent, or becoming well known due to one's talent, but rather merely being discovered for who you are and becoming famous. Being famous or infamous has become the end goal. This change is very important in the psyche of those who have internalized this expectation. The metaphors of *fame is good* or *success is fame* or *success is fame for one's talent* or *labor versus success is fame for being you* are important in how they affect the lives of our children.

The Impact of This Confluence on the Emerging Metaphor

When you mix together these elements you find that during the past 20 years or so, the primary metaphor influencing the perceptions of children with gifts and talents has become *life as entertainment* (Kövecses, 2005). At different times in American history, important metaphors for the purpose of life have included survival, self-improvement, gaining wealth, and now entertainment. Underpinning most of the dominant metaphors during the past 75 years has been the construct of a meritocracy. In a meritocracy, people earn and realize opportunities due to hard work and commitment to improving oneself. The emerging entertainment metaphor does not seem to be underpinned by such assumptions or concerns. Hence, being discovered means to become famous for the person one is, not based on any specific dedicated behaviors, sacrifices, or even goals.

Another aspect important to the entertainment metaphor is the ongoing expectation to be engaged in something one considers entertainment. Many children listen to music, watch television, and communicate with others on the computer, all while engaged in other endeavors. In other words, old notions of personality types determining who multitasks seem antiquated, being replaced by interests, passions, talent, access to technology, and the ever-present root metaphor of entertainment as a way of understanding life.

As adults interested in the development of gifted students, we will need to help shape the evolving characteristics of the entertainment metaphor to be sure that hard work, the importance of preparedness, goal setting, the role of incremental progress, stretching oneself, and occasional failure become internalized by our children. We also should commit to expanding students' knowledge base about professions and the pathways to get there. Because the entertainment metaphor seems more representative of our youth, we will need to recognize the fact that we cannot eliminate it, but we may be able to help define it. As we all live in an increasingly *me*-oriented society, building community will necessarily be on the terms of the children who understand their world with an entertainment metaphor as its basis. It is important that we come to understand both the ramifications of this metaphor and the meaning that it holds for our children in order for us to be effective shepherds (yet another metaphor) as we attempt to guide them successfully into adulthood.

FOR DISCUSSION

- What other metaphors can you think of that might be impacting the psychosocial development of students with gifts and talents?

- Discuss how you might be able to use the *life as entertainment* metaphor to achieve educational goals with gifted students.

CHAPTER 30

Changing Times

KEY CONCEPTS

- Stable and transitional factors in cultural definitions
- Margaret Mead's concepts of postfigurative, cofigurative, and prefigurative culture
- Disintermediation

In a previous chapter, "Gifted Students' Social and Emotional Development in the 21st Century," I attempted to illustrate some of the ways in which the lives of gifted students today are significantly different from those of previous generations. Later in that chapter, I made a plea to adults to understand that growing up in a time not experienced by previous generations requires us to act in ways that are not necessarily the ways we think we should. In this chapter, I continue the theme by drawing on the works of the very famous anthropologist Margaret Mead, as well as from some lesser known contemporary authors.

As a researcher interested in how we can guide gifted children's development in the psychological realm to help them become as healthy, happy, and successful as possible, I often read other scholars' accounts of where we are as a nation and world, where we have been, and where we are going. From my readings, I try to select the meaningful ideas from the less meaningful. I have come to believe in a few relatively stable factors, some variables in transition, and some important variables that are changing rapidly in important ways.

The first rather stable factor is that the United States is made up of a large number of cities, towns, and hamlets, with untold numbers of ghettos, communities, and villages. Across this array of living conditions are the myriad other ways people vary (e.g., ethnically, racially, religiously, regionally). Hence, when we think of the lives of our gifted students, we have to acknowledge that there is no one United States per se, but instead we have hundreds of differing influences factoring into the specifics of the lived experience of being gifted as an American. The specifics of the experience can be put under a loose interpretation of the culture in which a person lives.

An example of an important convention cutting across the enormous variation in the United States that has a significant impact on gifted children's lives (perhaps not equally, however) is the institution of marriage. At the same time as the divorce rate has changed in the U.S., there has also appeared a change in the manifestations of the nuclear family that includes increasing numbers of hybrid families and single-parent homes. There are some obvious and some less obvious outcomes of these types of changes on the psychological well-being of gifted students.

The next important factor is an example of a variable in transition. I include Mead's description of how our society has been evolving over the past generations. In 1970, Margaret Mead described a new cultural trend born of the technological changes of the past century. She noted that early cultures were easily transmitted from generation to generation because individuals always lived close to home. Three generations—children, parents, and grandparents—existed together in the same place. She called this a *postfigurative* culture, and in it a child's life would be predictably like that of his or her grandparents. As travel increased and young people moved away from their families, children's lives no longer mirrored their grandparents' lives, so the young people looked to their peers or other adults for cultural definition. Therefore, according to Mead, in this *configurative* culture, young people rely on the experience of their elders to a point; but, after that, they must learn from the members of their new place how to fit in. Mead claimed that advances in technology have made Americans immigrants both in place (as we have become a transient society) and in time (as our world has changed so rapidly through technology). Hence, our new *prefigurative* culture must create its own society without a dependence on the experiences of our elders. Mead (1970) described an erroneous assumption adults often hold about their own and subsequent generations:

It is assumed by the adult generation that there still is general agreement about the good, the true, and the beautiful, and that human nature, complete with built-in ways of perceiving, thinking, feeling, and acting, is essentially constant. Such beliefs are, of course, wholly incompatible with a full appreciation of the findings of anthropology, which has documented the fact that innovations in technology and in the form of institutions inevitably bring about alterations in cultural character. It is astonishing to see how readily a belief in change can be integrated with a belief in changelessness, even in cultures whose members have access to voluminous historical records and who agree that history consists not merely of currently desirable constructs but of verifiable facts. (p. 60)

There is a third category of important and rapidly changing factors from Mead's quote. The growth of the personal computer, generally, and the emergence of the Internet, specifically, are illustrating an important example of what Mead claimed more than 30 years ago: "innovations in technology and in the form of institutions inevitably bring about alterations in cultural character" (p. 60). An early example of this type of effect can be found in the South. Numerous books have been written about Southern hospitality, particularly as it pertains to impromptu social interactions on sidewalks, porches, streets, and the like. Once, where people crossed paths, a gracious interaction took place. With the new technology of air conditioning came fewer outdoor interactions of both strangers and friends alike. The effect of two generations having grown up with air conditioning has changed some of the cultural expectations for what it is to be Southern. Over time, these cultural expectations will be lost, to a large extent because of the effects of technology.

A more contemporary example of technology affecting our culture is still relatively early in its development. It is the overall effect of relying on computers for several types of activities that have typically required social interactions among various groups of people. Arguably, the most developed of these types of activities is the purchasing of products or services using the Internet. The most noticeable aspect of the development of the Internet over the past 5 years has been its commercialization. Monumental efforts to make available all types of products for purchase have seemingly driven the development of the Internet. Everything from automobiles to gambling opportunities can be purchased while sitting in one's home. These are ingredients for cultural change: opportunity, control, anonymity, and convenience.

In a 2000 lecture, software engineer and author Ellen Ullman described the marketing term *disintermediation* as a goal for businesses intent on using the Internet to separate the purchaser from everything except what is being bought. Disintermediation establishes the single consumer sitting at home, often alone, as the most powerful force in purchasing. To accomplish this goal, advertisers have marketed such concepts as this one, found on the billboard of a San Francisco theater: "Now the world really does revolve around you." Ullman went on to claim that the effects of this technology and marketing over time promote the "my" mentality in a very powerful way: "the 'My Computer' icon bothers me on the Windows desktop, baby names like 'My Yahoo' and 'My Snap'; my, my, my; 2-year-old talk; infantilizing and condescending" (p. 31). Advertising slogans such as "Wouldn't you rather be at home?" along with rapid advancements in technology have been projected to lead to a total individualization of experiences. For example, Ullman cited a museum owner's comments that extensive art holdings accessible through the Internet will soon lead to people establishing exhibits that only represent their personal interests. Her example, "Today I visited the museum of me. I liked it," is indicative of the wave about to affect our society.

Innumerable outcomes will potentially arise from this shift to the individual as the most valued consumer. One outcome includes the idea that civil space will no longer be needed and that the only place to find pleasure and satisfaction will be your home. As adults needing to guide gifted children, we must appreciate the substantial diverse makeup of the United States, understand the changes in family structures in ways that honor the natural diversity that comes from cultural evolution, and learn what we can in the general arena of technology. With this wisdom we should be able to accommodate the ever-changing social and emotional needs of all children, including gifted children.

FOR DISCUSSION

- Discuss how changes in family structures may impact the psychological well-being of gifted students.

- Margaret Mead noted that "It is astonishing to see how readily a belief in change can be integrated with a belief in changelessness." Comment on this in relation to giftedness and school systems.

- Provide further examples of how technology has influenced cultural traditions or expectations.

CHAPTER 31

Top 10 (Plus or Minus Two) List for the 20th Century

KEY CONCEPTS

- Psychometrically based pedagogy

- The influence of Binet, Terman, Freud, Watson, Thorndike, Skinner, Gardner, and Sternberg on gifted education

- The influence of Sputnik launch, Civil Rights laws, Public Law 94-142, learning theory, brain-based research, Jacob K. Javits legislation, the National Research Center on the Gifted and Talented, and changing U.S. demographics on gifted education

The following represents ideas about some of the most influential events, circumstances, and decisions to affect gifted education over the past 100 years. Some of the events are well known, while others may not be. Some of the circumstances reflect the world according to Tracy, while others are quite possibly part of history that has been, or one day will be, written about. Some of the decisions represent my take on them and may be arguable as facts, while others may represent a consensus in the field. In short, the ideas expressed here may not represent the folks at *Gifted Child Today*, Prufrock Press, or any other living, breathing person. They have been fun to think about, and the process has helped me clarify some of the underpinnings on which I base other ideas. Although I doubt that this list will become a historical road map for the field of gifted education, I hope it becomes an impetus for others to ponder this subject.

One of the assumptions I operated under while working on my list was that, because I knew that a couple of very capable thinkers were working on the same assignment, there would probably be some overlap in our lists. Consequently, I used that assumption to take some liberties with the charge. In a final prefacing comment, I would like to note that, once given this assignment by Dr. Susan Johnsen, I started generating items for top 10 lists. I worked on this by carrying around a pad and pencil for a couple of months. To date, I have created 14 different top 10 lists. I even lost one. A few of the lists were created as I woke up in the middle of the night, having had what I thought at the time was an epiphany. Several of those lists were ripped to shreds, burned, and then buried. So much for the creativity of my unconscious mind! This list is really an amalgam of ideas that seemed to reappear across the numerous lists generated or seemed to reflect ideas that might not get me drummed out of the field if I actually wrote them down. To make my thinking understandable in an efficient manner, I will tie together ideas that I believe are indicators and/or examples of the point I am trying to make. By explaining them, they may appear to be discrete from each other. In many cases, however, the ideas are connected, and in some cases, one idea sets the stage for the next, but not necessarily in a planned way. One final wringing of hands: My way of thinking is highly contextually driven. Consequently, the ideas will not be as detailed as I tend to imagine them.

Rather than count down from 10 to 1, I will offer a set of 10 (or so), starting with events in the late 1800s. I will call this set of events "From the Apgar Score to the Licensing Exam," or "The Reign of Standardized Testing." Better yet, number 10 is the emergence of efficient ways for making important educational decisions. Let me use the phrase *psychometrically based pedagogy*. I will credit the development of the Binet intelligence test as the earliest influence on gifted education. From Binet came the Army Alpha and Beta tests, the Stanford Binet, the Wechsler series, and a host of other efforts to measure a person's intellectual ability (and everything else about him or her, as well). The efficiency of group intelligence tests allowed decisions to be made in a highly time-efficient manner that, in my mind, set the standard for high-stakes testing. For example, doing poorly on the Army tests increased one's chances of going to the front during World War I as a foot soldier, where they died at a higher rate than those in other positions. The attitude was created, or at least reflected, in these practices that psychometric principles should be the basis for making hard decisions about young people's roles and responsibilities in the United States.

From this period also emerged the original Terman (1925) studies on intelligence. His work reflected the science and views of people of the era, yielding arguably the single most important study underpinning the field of gifted education today. Although it is unfair and anachronistic to hold Terman's research to all of the considerations and criteria of research conducted today, it is a fair statement that some in the field of gifted education have determined that the Terman research is quite limited in its representation of the many conceptions of giftedness popular today. Even with these concerns, I believe that the influence of the Terman research on today's ideas of giftedness cannot be overestimated. The research also added support for the use of standardized intelligence tests and gave support to the conception of giftedness. Moreover, the term IQ has become so ingrained in the American vernacular and psyche that groups of adults belong to clubs based on their IQ test scores. The last name of Albert Einstein has become synonymous with a high IQ score. "He's no Einstein" is a criticism often used to describe people thought to be dull.

During this time in history, Sigmund Freud was quite prominent in influencing beliefs about the nature of people. Although his views are both interesting and insightful, they did little to help the relatively young public school system accommodate the increasing numbers of immigrant children needing, expecting, and being forced to participate in schooling. Fortunately for the schools, John Watson and Edward Thorndike were setting the stage for Fred (a.k.a. B. F.) Skinner to provide some of the underpinnings needed to educate vast numbers of children from modest means. Skinner, Thorndike, and other behaviorists reified the concepts of a type of psychology and became the architects of mass schooling. Although Terman's influence helped establish an entity notion of giftedness—that giftedness is a thing that can be measured—the behaviorists influenced later writers to think that looking at the behaviors of children is a more important concern than relying on paper-and-pencil tests. The behaviorist view of teaching and learning required teachers to teach from the smallest concept to the larger idea by chaining. More importantly, however, behaviorists' mechanistic views of humankind challenged our basic core beliefs about people. Behaviors are learned; therefore, giftedness can be influenced. With these ideas, the early seeds were sown to add environmental influences to our prevailing concept of genius. Clearly, despite the fact that early philosophers had already espoused both positions, their influence was not so great as that of the philosopher psychologists in the first half of the 20th century.

In 1957, the Russians launched Sputnik. From all accounts, this event led the United States to begin an aggressive effort to catch up with the Russians in the space race. Of course, the Cold War and the fear that the Russians would dominate the world fueled this race. From this single event, numerous national, state, and local efforts to better prepare students in math and science were begun. For several years, educating students in mathematical and scientific areas seemed to be a high priority for the U.S. Prior to this period and for many years following it, Albert Einstein was one of the most recognized and respected people in the world. His popularity was that of a celebrity—the Michael Jordan of the era. Children aspired to be like Einstein.

In the 1960s, a cultural and Civil Rights revolution was in full force. From fashion, to political attitudes, to one's very personal aspirations, ideals were changing. Dr. Martin Luther King, Jr., Rosa Parks, and many others sought to bring to all people the same opportunities as those enjoyed by the people who had maintained power since the early years of the country. The Civil Rights Law, passed in 1964, signaled what I believe to be one of the three most important influences on gifted education. Although it is hard to imagine, prior to 1964, and to some extent today, children of color had been left out of educational efforts to maximize talent.

The next event that has had a significant impact on gifted education was the passage of Public Law 94–142 in 1974. This law effectively required schools to provide appropriate educational services to students with disabilities. When one reviews the history of public schools in the United States, few single events have had more impact on overall school practices throughout the U.S. than this law. Although I am somewhat disappointed that gifted students did not become a protected group as a direct result of this law, I believe the law's influence on the American understanding of education and the responsibility we have to accommodate the needs of exceptional students did have a tremendous impact on the lives of gifted students.

Between 1974 and today, one topic (conceptions of intelligence) has been widely written about both in the popular press and scholarly journals. The articles have had a tremendous impact on educators' thinking and, to a large extent, have pushed along our notions of giftedness. Although many of the contemporary notions of giftedness are not limited to an intelligence-based foundation, the field of gifted education is both underpinned by and somewhat held hostage to populists' notions of intelligence. In 1983, the book *Frames of Mind* by Howard Gardner was published. Soon thereafter, another view of intelligence by Robert Sternberg was published. Since the mid-1980s, numerous views have emerged. This public debate has been broad, with public school educators leading the way. It was clear that our traditional IQ-based notion of intelligence was too narrow to reflect the experiences of our nation's educators. Nothing was more powerful than an idea whose time had come. In essence, teachers were rejecting many psychologists' ideas about intelligence.

In a parallel theme that is more pervasive and yet subtler, public school teachers have been wrestling away from psychologists the mantle of defining what learning is and how it is done. Teachers had grown quite disillusioned with the touted research of famous psychologists about what should work with students in classrooms. After many years of being criticized for not teaching in ways that reflect researchers' ideas of teaching and learning, public school teachers have joined with philosophers and a different group of psychologists in claiming that students construct their understanding. This constructivist view of the world is popular among teachers and professors of education. Many learning theorists in psychology still maintain rather traditional views of how students learn. Those in society who determine the institutionally supported views of intelligence and learning theory are the most influential political groups in all of public education. For many years, the IQ-based definition of giftedness dominated the scene and was widely accepted by the general populace. However, since 1983, the de facto control over the application of definitions of intelligence (giftedness) and learning theory has ostensibly shifted from academics in universities to professional educators in public schools.

It will be fascinating over the next 20 years to monitor the most recent popular topic of research drawing considerable attention from researchers, professional educators, and lay-people alike: brain-based research. Although I am personally optimistic that important findings will be yielded from this line of research, we will undoubtedly have to live through periods of time when pedestrian notions of the research will affect classroom practices. For example, brain hemisphericity was the topic of many articles in the popular press some years ago, as were books on teaching to a child's right brain or left brain. This "movement" was so influential that teachers would describe children as "right-brained" or "left-brained."

The next major event reflects the evolution of pedagogy, changing from a rather inflexible practice of grade skipping to the various options that have been created over the past 40 years or so. Gifted education was not very appealing to parents and teachers when they worried that the only option for little Janie was for her to skip a grade or two. Today, teachers have myriad options for educating gifted students that include grade skipping, teaching techniques that attempt to differentiate the curriculum, and state-funded residential schools. Other options include Saturday and summer programs such as Governor's Schools, and various talent search programs.

Although the impetus behind these examples is quite different, I believe that the second option (differentiation) will continue to attract supporters among school personnel. The attraction of this option is that: (a) teachers are the primary decision makers when curricular differentiation is being implemented, and (b) it fits the inclusive model of education toward which many public schools are moving. Two important undercurrents to the support of an inclusion model of instruction are that it has a face validity of egalitarianism and that the term *gifted* is not used. Other historical events have accelerated the acceptance of differentiation. For example, after some early problems with the notion of gifted education, the middle school movement has warmed up to differentiation due to the relentless work of professionals like Carol Tomlinson who have made presentations at numerous conferences and written books that translate the tenets of differentiation into attractive language for general educators and administrators. Another factor important to this equation is the inclusion movement or having mixed-ability classrooms. Curricular differentiation makes great sense in heterogeneous classrooms.

Another recent event that has had an impact on gifted education has come from the confluence of several situations. The funding of Jacob K. Javits legislation and the subsequent birth of the National Research Center on the Gifted and Talented have brought increased attention to the needs of gifted students. Increased research and publications also have been an important by-product of these events. At the same time, the National Association for Gifted Children and the Council for Exceptional Children's division—The Association for the Gifted—have joined together to influence politicians about the nature and needs of gifted students. These two groups have also worked in collaboration with numerous other important professional educational groups to influence the national educational agenda relative to gifted education.

I believe that the changing demographic of people in the United States has had an important impact on gifted education over the past 20 years or so. I also believe that this influence will eventually have a greater impact on gifted education than will any other single event or circumstance. As the dominant group in our society that has been serviced directly by gifted education (i.e., Caucasian, middle-class males) grows ever smaller in the demographic equation, the other groups will have more power. Although the field of gifted education is still quite inadequate in applying some of the contemporary conceptions of giftedness, the issues surrounding these conceptions are being discussed, intellectual restlessness is present, and conflicting ideas are omnipresent. In essence, the stage has been set for many of the nontraditional ideas for defining giftedness, identifying gifted children, and providing services for them to be tested and researched. It will be interesting to see if another type of Civil Rights movement emerges driven by the notion of maximizing the school-related talent of all gifted children. If this type of movement gains momentum, I doubt that the way to resolve the historic disparities among groups of gifted children will be based on psychometric tweaking of instruments. Implicit in these comments is the argument that benefits made available to a society's children reflect the current power structure. Enhancing the opportunities for under-represented gifted children will require a type of revolution. Whether the field of gifted education has the ability or the will to change its practices so that they maximize all gifted children's abilities is doubtful. However, many bright, dedicated people from various backgrounds are working hard to bring about this change. Changing the basic structure of our schooling practices is a difficult thing to accomplish. Of course, the ground for proving many of these experiments may very well be in regular classroom settings.

I have chosen to end this chapter by cataloging some of the other trends and issues that I expect to have an effect on the direction and progress of the field of gifted education over the next 50 years. Other mediating trends may include: our confused notions of what giftedness is; the nation's economy; site-based management; individual school boards; national legislation; the evolution of computers and their effect on the practices of schooling; the politicization of schooling; and the goals of schooling. I think the goals we hold for our schools are largely met. I believe that if we truly expected our schools to maximize the potential of all gifted students by educating people who can function well in a democracy, many aspects of our schools would change. Because our society holds confused views about gifted students, gifted students necessarily receive mixed messages every day of their lives. The people who hold these confused views include those from all walks of life, from architects, to physicians, to teachers, to teacher trainers, and even to the gifted students themselves. I believe that until a coherent message about giftedness can be crafted that opens doors for the greatest number of gifted children, rather than letting only a very small number through, then society will remain discontented with schooling. Some prescribe a panacea of school choice as a remedy for their criticisms of our public schools. The criticisms are representative of one aspect of the problems with which schools struggle in trying to educate gifted students. That is, under this prescription, children are treated as commodities, as capital for our nation's economy. There is benefit to students becoming employable, but wouldn't it be nice if our goal was to educate people to be the best people they could be?

FOR DISCUSSION

- What do you believe are the most important events influencing pedagogical practices that have occurred over the past century?

CHAPTER 32

Disrupting Social Contracts That Affect Gifted Students: An Homage to "Harrison Bergeron"

- Social contract theory
- Equality and educational malfeasance

In 1961, Kurt Vonnegut wrote the short story "Harrison Bergeron" about America's quest for equality that had gone so far as to create a position of Handicapper General. This person's role was to create ways in which society could equalize the natural human variations so that everyone would be the same. To that end, dancers wore sandbags, great thinkers had severe electronic buzzers go off in their heads on a schedule based on how bright they were, and so forth. Great accomplishments were sacrificed so everyone could be the same.

Vonnegut's story can be instructive to those of us in gifted education. As we strive to avoid such handicaps being placed on the children to whom we are dedicated, how do we achieve the American goal of equality? We can examine this paradox through the lens of social contract theory.

The conception of social contract theory can be traced to the origins of the field of philosophy. Social contract theory (SCT) has evolved from Socrates all the way to modern-day philosophers. SCT represents the view that for societies to form and function, people must maintain political and moral obligations. A compelling case was made in the 1700's by Jean-Jacques Rousseau (1987) that social contracts ostensibly began when people moved from living as individuals in small groups in nature, to the time when property could be owned by individuals. He went on to claim that as populations increased and societies became increasingly complicated, and with the emergence of leisure time, comparisons among people became inevitable. Rousseau believed that these changes in society encouraged greed, competition, vanity, inequality, and so forth. He argued that as the initial inequalities of ownership expanded, societies became verticalized because so many people would be needed to work for the property owners to maintain their growing estates. Consequently, governments became increasingly focused on protecting the interests of landowners within a larger effort of representing the interests of all people. Unfortunately, according to Rousseau, the efforts to help all gave way to protection for the emerging wealthy class. Social contracts became the initial underpinning of Western civilization. The net effect of the evolution of the naturalized social contract is the root of the conflict and competition from which societies struggle.

Social contracts can range from political theory about the representative behavior of the individual that would be generalized to all, to the more immediate assumptions of life. The most foundational example of a social contract is the covenant formed by agreement that people will coexist under a set of rules in a conscious effort to live as a collective. Certain aspects of living within the community circumscribe absolute freedom of the individual so both the individual and the community can thrive. For example, within social contract theory, philosophical discussions have tried to illuminate what justice, fairness, and equity mean.

Rousseau (1987) worried about the effects on the individual to live within a system based on social contracts—that as some have amassed great wealth, most others have become limited by the social contracts into a subservient role. He believed that freedom and equality could be regained by exercising our free will through democratic ideals.

Modern-day social contracts relative to our students with gifts and talents warrant being reconsidered. For example, the uninformed and superficial understandings some people have regarding the meaning of equity have created impediments to students with gifts and talents. For many, equity means equal—it has been interpreted to mean "the same as." It is easy to trace this understanding to the concept of equality in the eyes of the law, typically meaning the same for everyone—everyone being held to the same (single) standard. Using that same understanding when thinking about the educational needs of students with gifts and talents creates an unnecessary limitation on their intellectual growth. Moreover, it can cause issues in their psychological well-being as well. In a common example, most states have interpreted No Child Left Behind (NCLB, 2001) as emphasizing the most basic/foundational skills (one standard), thus leaving gifted students unchallenged. As the former executive director of a state residential academy for intellectually gifted students, I found it was evident on a daily basis that in environments where gifted students can aspire beyond minimum competencies, they excel—in many cases well beyond what most people predict as possible. However, in traditional schools, gifted students are not challenged beyond the minimum standard. The net cost of retarding the intellectual development of gifted students is staggering to the United States. The sad irony in this example is that at the same time our schools are being attacked for poor performance on the part of its students, the same legislators who created NCLB are part of the social contract system that has supported a naïve egalitarian concept of schools that fosters working toward minimum standards. This has led to a second naïve set of goals to "close the achievement gap" among students. The potential performance variations among students should reveal considerable differences in achievement given the vast differences in intellectual potential. The clumsy approaches to narrow the achievement gap (fueled by the social contract of a fair and equitable school system) is to retard or at least neglect the growth of one group in society—gifted students—while emphasizing the growth of another—those struggling to reach the most basic of skills. Although no one would argue that we should leave struggling students behind, we certainly should not conspire to retard the development of another in order to claim the prize of equality. To disrupt this most important social contract between American citizens and schools, we should demand that our schools exist for one purpose: to maximize the potential of all students and not to merely meet minimum competencies. Then, meaningful subgoals would not hurt our students. Our current conceptions of fairness and equity have led us to a goal that has created social contracts and directed our resources to unintentionally cause harm to many of our most able students. We cannot continue to tolerate educational malfeasance under the flag of equality, nor should we continue to define equality down. Given the current social contracts, public policies, and school practices, we are only a step away from having a de facto Handicapper General who goes to great lengths to guarantee that everyone is exactly the same. Let us demand that equity be manifest, not in limiting some students so that a narrow range of achievement differences can be found, but rather to maximize the potential of all students, including those with gifts and talents.

FOR DISCUSSION

- Discuss the fairness of equity goals in our society.
- Why do some feel that accountability in our school system is a paramount goal? How does this goal affect students with gifts and talents?

REFERENCES

Allen, R. E. (Ed.). (1996). *The Reader's Digest Oxford complete wordfinder.* Pleasantville, NY: Reader's Digest Association.

Austin, J. H. (1978). *Chase, chance, and creativity.* New York, NY: Columbia University Press.

Bronfenbrenner, U. (1994). Ecological models of human development. In T. Husen & T. N. Postlethwaite (Eds.), *International encyclopedia of education* (2nd ed., Vol. 3, pp. 1643–1647). Oxford, England: Pergamon Press/ Elsevier Science.

Buescher, T. (1985). A framework for understanding the social and emotional development of gifted and talented students. *Roeper Review, 8,* 10–15.

Capuzzi, D., & Golden, L. (Eds.). (1988). *Preventing adolescent suicide.* Muncie, IN: Accelerated Development.

Coleman, L. J. (1985). *Schooling the gifted.* New York, NY: Addison Wesley.

Coleman, L. J., & Cross, T. L. (1988). Is being gifted a social handicap? *Journal for the Education of the Gifted, 11,* 41–56.

Coleman, L. J., & Cross, T. L. (2001). *Being gifted in school: An introduction to development, guidance, and teaching.* Waco, TX: Prufrock Press.

Costello, R. B. (Ed.). (1992). *Webster's college dictionary.* New York, NY: Random House.

Cross, T. L. (2001). Gifted children and Erikson's theory of psychosocial development. *Gifted Child Today, 24*(1), 54–55.

Cross, T. L., Coleman, L. J., & Terhaar-Yonkers, M. (1991). The social cognition of gifted students in schools: Managing the stigma of giftedness, *Journal for the Education of the Gifted, 15,* 44–55.

Cross, T., Cook, R., & Dixon, D. (1996). Psychological autopsies of three academically talented adolescents who committed suicide. *The Journal of Secondary Gifted Education, 7,* 403–409.

Davidson, L., & Linnoila, M. (1991). *Risk factors for youth suicide.* Washington, DC: National Institute of Mental Health.

Delisle, J. (1986). Death with honors: Suicide and the gifted adolescent. *Journal of Counseling and Development, 64,* 558–560.

Dweck, C. S. (1986). Motivation processes affecting learning. *American Psychologist, 41,* 1040–1048.

Dweck, C. S. (2008). *Mindset: The new psychology of success.* New York, NY: Ballantine.

Ebert, B. (1987). Guide to conducting a psychological autopsy. *Professional Psychology: Research and Practice, 18,* 52–56.

Erikson, E. H. (1963). *Childhood and society* (2nd ed.). New York, NY: Norton.

Erikson, E. H. (1972). Autobiographical notes on the identity crisis. In G. Holton (Ed.), *The twentieth-century sciences: Studies in the biography of ideas.* New York, NY: Norton.

Favazza, A. R. (1996). *Bodies under siege: Self-mutilation and body modification in culture and psychiatry.* Baltimore, MD: Johns Hopkins University Press.

Fox, C., & Hawton, K. (2004). *Deliberate self-harm in adolescence.* London, England: Jessica Kingsley.

Gardner, H. (1983). *Frames of mind: The theory of multiple intelligences.* New York, NY: BasicBooks.

Goffman, E. (1963). *Stigma: Notes on the management of spoiled identity.* Englewood Cliffs, NJ: Prentice Hall.

Hall, G. S. (1904). *Adolescence: Its psychology and its relations to physiology, anthropology, sociology, sex, crime, religion, and education.* New York, NY: Appleton.

Holinger, P. C., Offer, D., Barter, J. T., & Bell, C. C. (1994). *Suicide and homicide among adolescents.* New York, NY: Guilford.

Howley, C. B., Howley, A., & Pendarvis, E. D. (1995). *Out of our minds: Anti-intellectualism and talent development in American schooling.* New York, NY: Teachers College Press.

Izard, C. E., & Ackerman, B. P. (2000). Motivational, organizational, and regulatory function of discrete emotions. In M. Lewis & J. Heviland-Jones (Eds.), *Handbook of emotions* (2nd ed., pp. 253–264). New York, NY: Guilford.

Jones, D. (1977). Suicide by aircraft: A case report. *Aviation, Space, and Environmental Medicine, 48,* 454–459.

Kaiser, C. F., & Berndt, D. J. (1985). Predictors of loneliness in the gifted adolescent. *Gifted Child Quarterly, 29,* 74–77.

Katz, J. (2001). *Voices from the hellmouth.* Retrieved from http://slashdot.org/articles/99/04/25/1438249.shtml

Kövecses, Z. (2005). *Metaphor in culture: Universality and variation.* Cambridge, England: Cambridge University Press.

Kozol, J. (1991). *Savage inequalities: Children in America's schools.* New York, NY: Crown.

Lakoff, G., & Johnson, M. (1980). *Metaphors we live by.* Chicago, IL: University of Chicago Press.

LifeSIGNS. (2007). *Self-injury guidance and network support.* Retrieved from http://www.selfharm.org/what/precursors.html

Ludwig, A. L. (1995). *The price of greatness: Resolving the creativity and madness controversy.* New York, NY: Guilford.

May, R. (1969). The emergence of existential psychology. In R. May (Ed.), *Existential psychology* (pp. 1–48). New York, NY: Random House.

Mead, M. (1970). *Culture and commitment.* Garden City, NY: Natural History Press.

Mendaglio, S. (2007). Affective-cognitive therapy for counseling gifted individuals. In S. Mendaglio & J. S. Peterson (Eds.), *Models of counseling gifted children, adolescents and young adults* (pp. 35–68). Waco, TX: Prufrock Press.

Mendaglio, S. (2008). Dabrowski's Theory of Positive Disintegration: A personality theory for the 21st century. In S. Mendaglio (Ed.), *Dabrowski's theory of personality* (pp.13–40). Scottsdale, AZ: Great Potential Press.

Neill, K., Benensohn, H., Farber, A., & Resnick, H. (1974). The psychological autopsy: A technique for investigating a hospital suicide. *Hospital and Community Psychiatry, 25,* 33–36.

No Child Left Behind Act, 20 U.S.C. §6301 (2001).

Offer, D., & Offer, J. B. (1975). *From teenage to young manhood.* New York, NY: BasicBooks.

Piechowski, M. (1979). Developmental potential. In N. Colangelo & T. Zaffron (Eds.), *New voices in counseling the gifted* (pp. 25–57). Dubuque, IA: Kendall/Hunt.

Prensky, M. (2001). Digital natives, digital immigrants. *On the Horizon, 9*(5), 1, 3–6.

Rousseau, J. (1987). *The basic political writings* (D. A. Cress, Trans.) Indianapolis, IN: Hackett.

Salovey, P., & Mayer, J. D. (1990). Emotional intelligence. *Imagination, Cognition & Personality, 9,* 185–211.

Subotnik, R. F., & Jarvin, L. (2005). Beyond expertise: Conceptions of giftedness as great performance. In R. J. Sternberg & J. E. Davidson (Eds.), *Conceptions of giftedness* (2nd ed., pp. 343–357). New York, NY: Cambridge University Press.

Tannenbaum, A. J. (1983). *Gifted children: Psychological and educational perspectives.* New York, NY: MacMillan.

Terman, L. M. (1925). *Genetic studies of genius: Vol. 1. Mental and physical traits of a thousand gifted children.* Stanford, CA: Stanford University Press.

Tomlinson-Keasey, C., & Keasey, B. (1988). "Signatures" of suicide. In D. Capuzzi & L. Golden (Eds.), *Preventing adolescent suicide* (pp. 213–245). Muncie, IN: Accelerated Development.

Ullman, E. (2000, May). Wouldn't you rather be at home? The Internet and the myth of the powerful self. *Harper's,* 30–33.

Vanderhoff, H., & Lynn, S. J. (2001). The assessment of self-mutilation: Issues and clinical considerations. *Journal of Threat Assessment, 1,* 91–109.

Vonnegut, K., Jr. (1961, October). Harrison Bergeron. *Magazine of Fantasy and Science Fiction,* 5–10.

Winner, E. (1988). *The point of words: Children's understanding of metaphor and irony.* Cambridge, MA: Harvard University Press.

RESOURCES

Gifted Education Journals and Publications

Gifted Child Quarterly
Carolyn M. Callahan, Editor
Curry School of Education
University of Virginia
Ruffner Hall 282
Charlottesville, Virginia
Phone: (434) 924-0791
E-mail: cmc@virginia.edu
Website: http://gcq.sagepub.com

Gifted Child Today
Susan Johnsen, Editor
Department of Educational Psychology
Baylor University
One Bear Place 97301, Burleson 216
Waco, TX 76798
Telephone: (254) 710-6116
E-mail: Susan_Johnsen@baylor.edu
Website: http://journals.prufrock.com/
IJP/b/gifted-child-today

Gifted Education Communicator
Karen Daniels, Editor
9278 Madison Avenue
Orangevale, CA 95662
Phone: (916) 988-3999
Fax: (916) 988-5999
E-mail: cagoffice@aol.com
Website: http://www.cagifted.org

Gifted and Talented International
Taisir Subhi Yamin, Editor
Scientific Director
International Centre for Innovation in Education (ICIE-Paris)
Website: https://journal.world-gifted.org

Journal for the Education of the Gifted
Tracy L. Cross, Editor
Center for Gifted Education
The College of William and Mary
427 Scotland Street
Williamsburg, VA 23185
Phone: (757) 221-2362
E-mail: tlcross@wm.edu
Website: http://journals.prufrock.com/IJP/b/
journal-for-the-education-of-the-gifted

Journal of Advanced Academics (formerly the
Journal of Secondary Gifted Education)
Del Siegle and D. Betsy McCoach, Co-Editors
University of Connecticut
2131 Hillside Road, Unit 3007
Storrs, CT 06269
Phone: (860) 486-8759
Fax: (860) 486-2900
E-mail: jaa@uconn.edu
Website: http://www.gifted.uconn.edu/jaa

Parenting for High Potential
Jennifer Jolly, Editor
Department of Educational Theory, Policy, and Practice
Louisiana State University
201 Peabody Hall
Baton Rouge, LA 70803
Phone: (225) 578-2049
Fax: (225) 578-9135
E-mail: jollyphp@gmail.com
Website: http://www.nagc.org

Roeper Review
Don Ambrose, Editor
Graduate Department, School of Education
College of Liberal Arts, Education, and Sciences
Rider University
2083 Lawrenceville Road
Lawrenceville, NJ 08648
Phone: (609) 895-5647
E-mail: ambrose@rider.edu
Website: http://www.roeper.org/RoeperInstitute/roeperReview

Teaching for High Potential
Jeff Danielian, Editor
NAGC
1707 L Street, NW, Suite 550
Washington, DC 20036
Phone: (202) 785-4268
Fax: (202) 785-4248
E-mail: jdanielian@nagc.org
Website: http://www.nagc.org

Understanding Our Gifted
Dorothy Knopper, Publisher
Open Space Communications
P.O. Box 18268
Boulder, CO 80308
Phone: (303) 444-7020
Fax: (303) 545-6505
E-mail: dorothy@opensapcecomm.com
Website. http://www.our gifted.com

United States National Gifted Associations

American Association for Gifted Children (AAGC)
Margaret Evans Gayle, Executive Director
Duke University
P.O. Box 90359
Durham, NC 27708
Phone: (919) 783-6152
Website: http://www.aagc.org

Council for Exceptional Children (CEC)
Bruce Ramirez, Executive Director
1110 N. Glebe Road, Suite 300
Arlington, VA 22201
Phone: (888) 232-7733
TTY: (866) 915-5000
Fax: (703) 264-9494
E-mail: service@cec.sped.org
Website: http://www.cec.sped.org

The Association for the Gifted (TAG)
Susan Johnsen, President
Department of Educational Psychology
Baylor University
One Bear Place 97304, Burleson 216
Waco, TX 76798
Phone: (254) 710-6116
E-mail: Susan_Johnsen@baylor.edu
Website: http://www.cectag.org

National Association for Gifted Children (NAGC)
Ann Robinson, President
1331 H Street, NW, Suite 1001
Washington, DC 20005
Phone: (202) 785-4268
Fax: (202) 785-4248
E-mail: nagc@nagc.org
Website: http://www.nagc.org

The National Foundation for Gifted and Creative Children (NFGCC)
395 Diamond Hill Road
Warwick, RI 02886
Phone: (401) 738-0937
Website: http://www.nfgcc.org

Supporting Emotional Needs of the Gifted (SENG)
Rosina Gallagher, President
P.O. Box 488
Poughquag, NY 12570
Phone: (845) 797-5054
E-mail: office@sengifted.org
Website: http://www.sengifted.org

Centers for Gifted Education

Center for Creative Learning
Don Treffinger, President
Center for Creative Learning, Inc.
4921 Ringwood Meadow
Sarasota, FL 34235
Phone: (941) 342-9928
Fax: (941) 342-0064
E-mail: Info@CreativeLearning.com
Website: http://www.creativelearning.com

The Center for Gifted
Joan Franklin Smutny, Director
National-Louis University
1926 Waukegan Road, Suite 2
Glenview, IL 60025
Phone: (847) 901-0173
Fax: (847) 901-0179
E-mail: info@centerforgifted.org
Website: http://www.centerforgifted.org

Center for Gifted Education
University of Arkansas at Little Rock
Dickinson Hall
2801 South University Avenue
Little Rock, AR 72204
Phone: (501) 569-3410
Website: http://giftedctr.ualr.edu

Center for Gifted Education
Dr. Sally Dobyns, Director
University of Louisiana–Lafayette
Maxim Doucet Hall, Room 107
Lafayette, LA 70504
Phone: (337) 482-6701
Fax: (337) 482-5842
E-mail: sdobyns@louisiana.edu
Website: http://www.coe.louisiana.edu/centers/gifted.html

Center for Gifted Education
Margo Long, Director
Whitworth College
Dixon Hall
300 W. Hawthorne Road
Spokane, WA 99251
Phone: (509) 777-3226
E-mail: gifted@whitworth.edu
Website: http://www.whitworth.edu/Academic/Department/
Education/Gifted

The Center for Gifted Education
Tracy L. Cross, Executive Director
College of William and Mary
P.O. Box 8795
Williamsburg, VA 23187
Phone: (757) 221-2362
Fax: (757) 221-2184
E-mail: cfge@wm.edu
Website: http://www.cfge.wm.edu

The Center for Gifted Studies
Julia Roberts, Director
Western Kentucky University
1906 College Heights Boulevard
Bowling Green, KY 42101-1031
Phone: (270) 745-5591
Fax: (270) 745-6279
E-mail: gifted@wku.edu
Website: http://www.wku.edu/Dept/Support/AcadAffairs/Gifted

Center for Gifted Studies and Talent Development
Cheryll M. Adams, Director
Ball State University
Burris Lab School 109
2201 W. University Avenue
Muncie, IN 47306
Phone: (765) 285-5390
Fax: (765) 285-3783
E-mail: cadams@bsu.edu
Website: http://www.bsu.edu/gifted

Center for Talent Development
Paula Olszewski-Kubilius, Director
School of Education and Social Policy
Northwestern University
617 Dartmouth Place
Evanston, IL 60208
Phone: (847) 491-3782
Fax: (847) 467-4283
E-mail: ctd@northwestern.edu
Website: http://www.ctd.northwestern.edu/ctd

Center for Talented Youth (CTY)
Lea Ybarra, Executive Director
Johns Hopkins University
McAuley Hall
5801 Smith Avenue, Suite 400
Baltimore, MD 21209
Phone: (410) 735-4100
Fax: (410) 735-6200
E-mail: ctyinfo@jhu.edu
Website: http://cty.jhu.edu

Centre for Gifted Education
University of Calgary
Education Tower, Room 602
2500 University Drive NW
Calgary, AB T2N 1N4
Phone: (403) 220-7799
Fax: (403) 210-2068
E-mail: gifted@ucalgary.ca
Website: http://gifted.ucalgary.ca

DISCOVER Projects
C. June Maker
Department of Special Education, Rehabilitation, & School
Psychology
College of Education
University of Arizona
Tucson, AZ 85721
Phone: (520) 622-8106
Fax: (520) 621-3821
E-mail: discover@email.arizona.edu
Website: http://discover.arizona.edu/index.html

Drury University Center for Gifted Education
Mary Potthoff, Director
Drury University
900 N. Benton Avenue
Springfield, MO 65802
Phone: (417) 873-7386
E-mail: mpotthof@drury.edu
Website: http://www.drury.edu/giftededucation

Duke University Talent Identification Program (TIP)
1121 West Main Street
Durham, NC 27701
Phone: (919) 668-9100
Fax: (919) 681-7921
E-mail: information@tip.duke.edu
Website: http://www.tip.duke.edu/index.html

The Frances A. Karnes Center for Gifted Studies
Frances A. Karnes, Director
University of Southern Mississippi
P.O. Box 8207
118 College Drive
Hattiesburg, MS 39406
Phone: (601) 266-5236; (601) 266-5246
Fax: (601) 266-4764
E-mail: gifted.studies@usm.edu
Website: http://www.usm.edu/gifted

Gifted Development Center
Linda Silverman
1452 Marion Street
Denver, CO 80218
Phone: (303) 837-8378
Fax: (303) 831-7465
E-mail: gifted@gifteddevelopment.com
Website: http://www.gifteddevelopment.com/index.htm

Gifted Education Resource Institute (GERI)
Marcia Gentry, Director
Purdue University
Beering Hall, Room 5108A
100 N. University Street
West Lafayette, IN 47907
Phone: (765) 494-7243
Fax: (765) 496-2706
E-mail: geri@purdue.edu
Website: http://www.geri.soe.purdue.edu

Leta Hollingworth Center for the Study and Education of the Gifted
Lisa R. Wright, Director
Teachers College
Columbia University
TC Box 170
309 Main Hall
525 W. 120th Street
New York, NY 10027
Phone: (212) 678-3851
E-mail: hollingworth@tc.columbia.edu
Website: http://www.tc.columbia.edu/centers/hollingworth

National Research Center on the Gifted and Talented (NRC/GT)
Curry School of Education
University of Virginia
Ruffner Hall
405 Emmet Street
Charlottesville, VA 22904
Phone: (434) 982-2849
E-mail: NRCGT@virginia.edu
Website: http://curry.edschool.virginia.edu/overview-gifted-277

Naeg Center for Gifted Education and Talent Development
University of Connecticut
2131 Hillside Road, Unit 3007
Storrs, CT 06269
Phone: (860) 486-4826
Fax: (860) 486-2900
Website: http://www.gifted.uconn.edu

Torrance Center for Creativity and Talent Development
Dr. Mark Runco, Director and the E. Paul Torrance Professor
323 Aderhold Hall
University of Georgia
Athens, GA 30602
Phone: (706) 542-5104
Fax: (706) 542-4659
E-mail: creative@uga.edu
Website: http://www.coe.uga.edu/Torrance

State Gifted Associations and Departments of Education

U.S. Department of Education
400 Maryland Avenue SW
Washington, DC 20202
Phone: (800) 872-5327
Fax: (202) 401-0689
Website: http://www.ed.gov/index.jhtml

Alabama

Alabama Association for Gifted Children (AAGC)
Patti Mizell, President
P.O. Box 43725
Birmingham, AL 35243
E-mail: pmizell@ocbe.k12.al.us
Website: http://www.alabamagifted.org

Alabama Department of Education
50 N. Ripley Street
P.O. Box 302101
Montgomery, AL 36104
Phone: (334) 242-9700
Website: http://www.alsde.edu/html/home.asp

Alaska

Alaska Department of Education and Early Development
P.O. Box 110500
801 W. 10th Street, Suite 200
Juneau, AK 99811
Phone: (907) 465-2800
Fax: (907) 465-4156
Website: http://www.eed.state.ak.us
Special Education Website: http://www.eed.state.ak.us/tls/sped

Arizona

Arizona Association for Gifted and Talented
P.O. Box 31088
Phoenix, AZ 85046
Phone: (602) 882-1848
Fax: (866)-693-3119
Website: http://www.arizonagifted.org

Arizona Department of Education
1535 W. Jefferson Street
Phoenix, AZ 85007
Phone: (602) 542-5393
Website: http://www.ade.state.az.us

Office of Gifted Education
Peter Laing, Director
Gifted Education/Advanced Placement Accountability Division
Phone: (602) 364-3842
Fax: (602) 542-5440
E-mail: Peter.Laing@azed.gov
Website: http://www.ade.state.az.us/asd/gifted

Arkansas

Arkansas Department of Education
4 Capitol Mall
Little Rock, AR 72201
Phone: (501) 682-4475
Website: http://arkansased.org

Gifted and Talented Education
Robin Clark, President
13 School Drive
Greenbrier, AR 72058
Phone: (501) 679-1060
Fax: (501) 679-1060
E-mail: clarkr@brier.k12.ar.us
Website: http://www.agate-arkansas.org

California

California Association for the Gifted (CAG)
9278 Madison Avenue
Orangevale, CA 95662
Phone: (916) 988-3999
Fax: (916) 988-5999
E-mail: cagoffice@aol.com
Website: http://www.cagifted.org

California Department of Education
1430 N Street
Sacramento, CA 95814
Phone: (916) 319-0800
Website: http://www.cde.ca.gov

Gifted and Talented Education (GATE)
George Olive
1430 N Street
Sacramento, CA 95814
Phone: (916) 323-8901
E-mail: golive@cde.ca.gov
Website: http://www.cde.ca.gov/sp/gt

Colorado

Colorado Association for Gifted and Talented
P.O. Box 460182
Aurora, CO 80046
Website: http://www.coloradogifted.org

Colorado Department of Education
201 E. Colfax Avenue
Denver, CO 80203
Phone: (303) 866-6600
Fax: (303) 830-0793
Website: http://www.cde.state.co.us

Gifted and Talented Services
Jacquelin Medina
Gifted Education Unit
Colorado Department of Education
201 East Colfax Avenue, Suite 300
Denver, CO 80203
Phone: (303) 866-6652
Fax: (303) 866-6599
E-mail: medina_j@cde.state.co.us
Website: http://www.cde.state.co.us/gt/index.htm

Connecticut

Connecticut Association for the Gifted (CAG)
P.O. Box 2598
Westport, CT 06880
Phone: (203) 291-6586
E-mail: info@ctgifted.org
Website: http://www.CTGifted.org

Connecticut State Department of Education
165 Capitol Avenue
P.O. Box 2219
Hartford, CT 06106
Phone: (860) 713-6543
Website: http://www.state.ct.us/sde

Gifted and Talented, Connecticut State Department of Education
Jeanne Purcell, Consultant
Bureau of Teaching and Learning
E-mail: jeanne.purcell@ct.gov
Phone: (860) 713-6745
Website: http://www.sde.ct.gov/sde/cwp/view.
asp?a=2618&q=320852

Delaware

Delaware Department of Education
John G. Townsend Building
401 Federal Street, Suite 2
Dover, DE 19901
Phone: (302) 735-4000
Fax: (302) 739-4654
Website: http://www.doe.k12.de.us

District of Columbia

State Education Office
810 First Street NE, 9th Floor
Washington, DC 20002
Phone: (202) 727-6436
E-mail: osse@dc.gov
Website: http://www.osse.dc.gov

Florida

Florida Association for the Gifted (FLAG)
Lauri Kirsch, President Pro Tem
Phone: (813) 215-6533 or (813) 272-4966
E-mail: lbkirsch@mindspring.com, lauri.kirsh@sdhc.k12.fl.us
Website: http://www.flagifted.org

Florida Gifted Network
Terry Wilson, Director
5101 Lake in the Woods Boulevard
Lakeland, FL 33813
Phone: (863) 647-3003
Fax: (425) 699-5560
E-mail: twilson@floridagiftednet.org
Website: http://www.floridagiftednet.org

Florida Department of Education
Commissioner Eric Smith
Turlington Building
325 W Gaines Street, Suite 1514
Tallahassee, FL 32399
Phone: (850) 245-0505
Fax: (850) 245-9667
Website: http://www.fldoe.org

Georgia

Georgia Association for Gifted Children
1579F Monroe Drive, #321
Atlanta, GA 30324
Phone/Fax: (404) 875-2284
Website: http://www.gagc.org

Georgia Department of Education
Brad Bryant, State Superintendent of Schools
2066 Twin Towers East
Atlanta, GA 30334
Phone: (404) 656-2800
Fax: (404) 651-8737
E-mail: state.superintendent@doe.k12.ga.us
Website: http://www.doe.k12.ga.us/index.aspx

Hawaii

Hawaii Department of Education
P.O. Box 2360
Honolulu, HI 96804
Phone: (808) 586-3230
Fax: (808) 586-3234
E-mail: doe_info@notes.k12.hi.us
Website: http://doe.k12.hi.us

Early Childhood/Gifted Education
Hawaii Gifted Association
1232 Waimanu Street E-1
Honolulu, HI 96814
Phone: (808) 597-8824

Idaho

Idaho—The Association for Gifted/State Advocates for Gifted Education (ITAG/SAGE)
2420 Spalding
Boise, ID 83705
Website: http://www.itag-sage.org

Idaho State Department of Education
650 W. State Street
P.O. Box 83720
Boise, ID 83720
Phone: (208) 332-6800
Fax: (208) 334-2228
Website: http://www.sde.idaho.gov/

Gifted and Talented
Dr. Val Schorzman, Coordinator
Phone: (208) 332-6920
E-mail: vjschorzman@sde.idaho.gov
Website: http://www.sde.idaho.gov/site/gifted_talented

Illinois

Illinois Association for Gifted Children
800 E. Northwest Hwy, Suite 610
Palatine, IL 60074
Phone: (847) 963-1892
Fax: (847) 963-1893
Website: http://www.iagcgifted.org

Illinois State Board of Education
100 N. First Street
Springfield, IL 62777
Phone: (866) 262-6663
Website: http://www.isbe.state.il.us

Indiana

Indiana Association for the Gifted (IAG)
P.O. Box 84
Whitestown, IN 46075
Phone/Fax: (317) 769-0187
E-mail: mail@iag-online.org
Website: http://www.iag-online.org/Indiana_Association_for_the_
Gifted/IAG_Home.html

Indiana Department of Education
151 West Ohio Street
Indianapolis, IN 46204
Phone: (317) 232-6610
Fax: (317) 232-8004
E-mail: webmaster@doe.in.gov
Website: http://www.doe.in.gov

Gifted and Talented Education
Office of High Ability Education
Indiana Department of Education
151 West Ohio Street
Indianapolis, IN 46204
Phone: (317) 232-0570
Fax: (317) 232-0589
E-mail: webmaster@doe.in.gov
Website: http://ideanet.doe.state.in.us/exceptional/gt

Iowa

Iowa Talented and Gifted Association (ITAG)
5619 NW 86th Street, Suite 600
Johnston, IA 50131
Phone: (515) 225-2323
Fax: (515) 327-5050
E-mail: itag@assoc-serv.com
Website: http://iowatag.org

Iowa Department of Education
Kevin Fangman, Acting Director
Grimes State Office Building
400E 14th Street
Des Moines, IA 50319
Phone: (515) 281-5294
Website: http://www.iowa.gov/educate

Kansas

Kansas Association for the Gifted, Talented, and Creative
Beverly Fink, President
E-mail: KGTC.president@gmail.com
Website: http://www.kgtc.org

Kansas Department of Education
120 SE 10th Avenue
Topeka, KS 66612
Phone: (785) 296-3201
Fax: (785) 296-7933
Website: http://www.ksde.org

Kentucky

Kentucky Association for Gifted Education (KAGE)
P.O. Box 9610
Bowling Green, KY 42102
Phone: (270) 745-4301
Fax: (270) 745-6279
E-mail: kage@wku.edu
Website: http://www.wku.edu/kage

Kentucky Department of Education
500 Mero Street
Frankfort, KY 40601
Phone: (502) 564-4770
TTY: (502) 564-4970
Website: http://www.kde.state.ky.us/KDE

Gifted and Talented Education Services
Greg Finkbonner
500 Mero Street, 18th Floor CPT
Frankfort, KY 40601
Phone: (502) 564-2106
E-mail: Greg.Finkbonner@education.ky.gov
Website: http://education.ky.gov/KDE/Instructional+Resources/
Gifted+and+Talented

Louisiana

Louisiana Department of Education
P.O. Box 94064
Baton Rouge, LA 70804
Phone: (877) 453-2721
Website: http://www.louisianaschools.net

Division of Special Populations
P.O. Box 94064
Baton Rouge, LA 70804
Phone: (225) 342-3513
E-mail: Susan.Batson@la.gov
Website: http://www.louisianaschools.net/lde/eia/home.html

Maine

Maine Department of Education
23 State House Station
Augusta, ME 04333
Phone: (207) 624-6600
Fax: (207) 624-6700
TTY: (888) 577-6690
Website: http://www.maine.gov/education

Gifted and Talented
Clifford McHatten
Gifted and Talented Education
Phone: (207) 624-6654
E-mail: GT.DOE@maine.gov
Website: http://www.maine.gov/education/gt/index.html

Maryland

Gifted and Talented Association of Montgomery County
Patricia O'Neill, Chair
308 Penwood Road
Silver Spring, MD 20901
Phone: (301) 593-1702
E-mail: communications@gtamc.org
Website: http://www.gtamc.org/Home

Maryland Department of Education
200 W. Baltimore Street
Baltimore, MD 21201
Phone: (410) 767-0600
Website: http://www.marylandpublicschools.org/msde

Gifted and Talented Education
Jeanne Paynter, Specialist
200 W. Baltimore Street
Baltimore, MD 21201
Phone: (410) 767-0363
Fax: (410) 333-2379
Website: http://www.marylandpublicschools.org/MSDE/programs/
giftedtalented

Massachusetts

Massachusetts Association for Gifted Education (MAGE)
Susan Dulong Langley, Chairperson
P.O. Box 1112
Framingham, MA 01701
E-mail: sdlangley@aol.com
Website: http://www.MASSGifted.org

Massachusetts Department of Education
75 Pleasant Street
Malden, MA 02148
Phone: (781) 338-3000
TTY: (800) 439-2370
Website: http://www.doe.mass.edu

Michigan

Michigan Alliance for Gifted Education (MAGE)
Ellen Fiedler, President
5355 Northland Drive NE, Suite C188
Grand Rapids, MI 49525
Phone: (616) 365-8230
Fax: (616) 364-1114
E-mail: ellenfiedler@comcast.net
Website: http://www.migiftedchild.org

Michigan Department of Education
608 W. Allegan Street
P.O. Box 30008
Lansing, MI 48909
Phone: (517) 373-3324
E-mail: mdeweb@michigan.gov
Website: http://www.michigan.gov/mde
Talent Development Website: http://www.michigan.gov/
mde/0,1607,7-140-6530_30334_40100---,00.html

Minnesota

Minnesota Council for the Gifted and Talented
5701 Normandale Road, Suite 315
Edina, MN 55424
Phone: (952) 848-4906
E-mail: info@mcgt.net
Website: http://www.mcgt.net

Minnesota Department of Children, Families, and Learning
1500 Highway 36 West
Roseville, MN 55113
Phone: (651) 582-8200
Website: http://cfl.state.mn.us/MDE/index.html

Gifted and Talented Education
Wendy Behrens, Specialist
Phone: (651) 582-8786
E-mail: wendy.behrens@state.mn.us
Website: http://cfl.state.mn.us/MDE/Academic_Excellence/Gifted_
and_Talented/index.html

Mississippi

Mississippi Department of Education
359 N. West Street
P.O. Box 771
Jackson, MS 39205
Phone: (601) 359-3513
E-mail: askmde@mde.k12.ms.us
Website: http://www.mde.k12.ms.us

Gifted Education
Chauncey Spears, Division Director,
Advanced Learning and Gifted Programs
359 N. West Street
Phone: (601) 359-2586
Fax: (601) 359-2040
E-mail: crspears@mde.k12.ms.us
Website: http://www.mde.k12.ms.us/acad/id/curriculum/gifted/
gifted.html

Missouri

Gifted Association of Missouri (GAM)
Website: http://www.mogam.org

Missouri Department of Elementary and Secondary Education
P.O. Box 480
Jefferson City, MO 65102
Phone: (573) 751-4212
Fax: (573) 751-8613
E-mail: pubinfo@dese.mo.gov
Website: http://dese.mo.gov

Gifted Education Programs
David Welch, Director
Phone: (573) 751-2453
E-mail: david.welch@dese.mo.gov
Website: http://dese.mo.gov/divimprove/gifted

Montana

Montana Association of Gifted and Talented Education
Tamara Fisher, President
E-mail: thethinkteacher@bomfuso.net
Website: http://www.mtagate.org

Montana Office of Public Instruction
Denise Juneau, Superintendent
P.O. Box 202501
Helena, MT 59620
Phone: (888) 231-9393
E-mail: OPISupt@mt.gov
Website: http://opi.mt.gov

Nebraska

Nebraska Association for the Gifted
John Thomsen, Communications Coordinator
2623 N. 145 Avenue
Omaha, NE 68116
E-mail: jthomsen2623@cox.net
Website: http://www.negifted.org

Nebraska Department of Education
301 Centennial Mall South
P.O. Box 94987
Lincoln, NE 68509
Phone: (402) 471-2295
Website: http://www.nde.state.ne.us

High Ability Learning
Mary Duffy
Phone: (402) 471-0737
E-mail: mary.duffy@nebraska.gov
Website: http://www.nde.state.ne.us/hal/hiabilitylrn.html

Nevada

Nevada Association for Gifted and Talented (NAGT)
Sue Gurlides, President
520 Joe Willis Street
Las Vegas, NV 889144
E-mail: susieq6459@aol.com

Nevada Department of Education
Keith W. Rheault, Superintendent of Public Instruction
700 E. Fifth Street
Carson City, NV 89701
Phone: (775) 687-9200
Fax: (775) 687-9101
Website: http://www.doe.nv.gov

SPED, ESEA & School Improvement
Rorie Fitz-Patrick, Director
Phone: (775) 687-9215
E-mail: rfitzpatrick@doc.nv.gov

New Hampshire

New Hampshire Association for Gifted Education (NHAGE)
Michele Munson, Director
P.O. Box 10432
Bedford, NH 03825
Phone: (603) 671-8800
E-mail: nhaged@yahoo.com
Website: http://www.nhage.org

New Hampshire Department of Education
101 Pleasant Street
Concord, NH 03301
Phone: (603) 271-3494
Fax: (603) 271-1953
Website: http://www.ed.state.nh.us/education/index.htm

Gifted and Talented Education
Kenneth J. Relihan
Phone: (603) 271-6151
Fax: (603) 271-7381
E-mail: krelihan@ed.state.nh.us
Website: http://www.education.nh.gov/instruction/curriculum/
gifted_talented/index.htm

New Jersey

New Jersey Association for Gifted Children (NJAGC)
P.O. Box 667
Mt. Laurel, NJ 08054
Phone: (856) 273-7530
Fax: (856) 829-5074
E-mail: njagc@njagc.org
Website: http://www.njagc.org

New Jersey Department of Education
P.O. Box 500
Trenton, NJ 08625
Phone: (877) 900-6960
Website: http://www.state.nj.us/education

New Mexico

New Mexico State Department of Education
Jerry Apodaca Education Building
300 Don Gaspar
Santa Fe, NM 87501
Phone: (505) 827-5800
Website: http://www.ped.state.nm.us

New York

Advocacy for Gifted and Talented Education in New York (AGATE)
Audrey Dowling, President
6439 South Portage Road
Westfield, NY 14787
E-mail: dowlings@fairpoint.net
Website: http://www.agateny.com

New York State Education Department
89 Washington Avenue
Albany, NY 12234
Phone: (518) 474-3852
Website: http://www.nysed.gov

North Carolina

North Carolina Association for the Gifted and Talented (NCAGT)
Wesley Guthrie, Executive Director
P.O. Box 899
Swansboro, NC 28584
Phone: (910) 326-8463
Fax: (910) 326-8465
E-mail: info@ncagt.org
Website: http://www.ncagt.org

North Carolina State Board of Education
301 North Wilmington Street
Raleigh, NC 27601
Phone: (919) 807-3300
Website: http://www.ncpublicschools.org/stateboard

Exceptional Children Division, Academically/Intellectually Gifted
Mary N. Watson, Director
E-mail: mwatson@dpi.state.nc.us
Website: http://www.dpi.state.nc.us/ec

North Dakota

North Dakota Department of Public Instruction
Dr. Wayne G. Sanstead, State Superintendent
600 E. Boulevard Avenue, Dept. 201
Bismarck, ND 58505
Phone: (701) 328-2260
E-mail: dpi@nd.gov
Website: http://www.dpi.state.nd.us

Ohio

Ohio Association for Gifted Children (OAGC)
Ann Sheldon, Director
P.O. Box 30801
Gahanna, OH 43230
Phone: (614) 337-0386
Fax: (614) 337-9286
E-mail: executivedirector@oagc.com
Website: http://www.oagc.com

Ohio Department of Education
25 S. Front Street
Columbus, OH 43215
Phone: (877) 644-6338
Website: http://www.ode.state.oh.us

Office for Exceptional Children
Kathe Shelby, Director
25 S. Front Street, Mail Stop 202
Columbus, Ohio 43215
Phone: (614) 466-2650
Fax: (614) 387-0968
E-mail: kathe.shelby@ode.state.oh.us
Website: http://education.ohio.gov/GD/Templates/Pages/ODE/
ODEDetail.aspx?page=3&TopicRelationID=967&ContentID=1184
3&Content=66256

Oklahoma

Oklahoma Association for Gifted, Creative, and Talented (OAGCT)
Dr. Linnea Van Eman, President
P.O. Box 721855
Norman, OK 73070
Phone: (888) 398-0250
E-mail: lve_ed2@sbcglobal.net
Website: http://oagct.org

Oklahoma State Department of Education
2500 N. Lincoln Boulevard
Oklahoma City, OK 73105
Phone: (405) 521-3301
Fax: (405) 521-6205
Website: http://sde.state.ok.us

Gifted and Talented Office
Cathy Douglas or Sara Austin
Phone: (405) 521-4287
Website: http://sde.state.ok.us/Curriculum/GiftTalent/default.html

Oregon

Oregon Association for Talented and Gifted (OATAG)
P.O. Box 1703
Beaverton, OR 97075
Phone: (206) 309-7265
E-mail: board@oatag.org
Website: http://www.oatag.org

Oregon Department of Education
255 Capitol Street NE
Salem, OR 97310
Phone: (503) 947-5600
Fax: (503) 378-5156
E-mail: ode.frontdesk@ode.state.or.us
Website: http://www.ode.state.or.us

Talented and Gifted
Rebecca Blocher, Specialist
Phone: (503) 947-5931 x75931
E-mail: Rebecca.Blocher@state.or.us
Website: http://www.ode.state.or.us/search/results/?id=76

Pennsylvania

Pennsylvania Association for Gifted Education (PAGE)
P.O. Box 15350
Pittsburg, PA 15350
Phone: (888) 736-6443
Website: http://www.giftedpage.org

Pennsylvania Department of Education
Thomas Gluck, Acting Secretary of Education
333 Market Street
Harrisburg, PA 17126
Phone: (717) 783-6788
Website: http://www.pde.state.pa.us

Gifted Education
Shirley Curl
Phone: (717) 786-6361
E-mail: scurl@state.pa.us
Website: http://www.portal.state.pa.us/portal/server.pt/community/
gifted_education/7393

Rhode Island

Rhode Island Advocates for Gifted Education (RIAGE)
Carolyn Rosenthal, Chair
P.O. Box 219
Barrington, RI 02806
E-mail: chaslyn@aol.com
Website: http://www.riage.org/index.html

Rhode Island Department of Elementary and Secondary Education
255 Westminster Street
Providence, RI 02903
Phone: (401) 222-4600
Website: http://www.ride.ri.gov/

Special Education: Talent Development
Kenneth Swanson, Director
Phone: (401) 222-3505
Website: http://www.ride.ri.gov/Special_Populations/Programs_
Services/Students_Learning_Beyond_Grade_Level.aspx

South Carolina

South Carolina Department of Education
1429 Senate Street
Columbia, SC 29201
Phone: (803) 734-8500
Fax: (803) 734-3389
E-mail: info@ed.sc.gov
Website: http://ed.sc.gov

Gifted and Talented
Rick Blanchard, Education Associate
1429 Senate Street, Room 802B
Columbia, SC 29201
Phone: (803) 734-8335
Fax: (803) 734-5953
E-mail: rblancha@ed.sc.gov
Website: http://ed.sc.gov/agency/Standards-and-Learning/
Academic-Standards/old/cso/gifted_talented/gt.html

South Dakota

South Dakota Association for Gifted Education
Rose Des Camps, President
Holgate Middle School
2200 North Dakota Street
Aberdeen, SD 57401
Phone: (605) 725-7723
E-mail: rose.descamps@k12.sd.us
Website: http://www.sd-agc.org

South Dakota Department of Education
800 Governor's Drive
Pierre, SD 57501
Phone: (605) 773-3134
Website: http://doe.sd.gov

Tennessee

Tennessee Association for the Gifted (TAG)
Leah Meulemans, President
E-mail: tag.leah@gmail.com
Website: http://www.tag-tenn.org

Tennessee Department of Education
Andrew Johnson Tower, 6th Floor
710 James Robertson Pkwy.
Nashville, TN 37243
Phone: (615) 741-2731
E-mail: education.comments@tn.gov
Website: http://www.tennessee.gov/education

Texas

Texas Association for the Gifted and Talented (TAGT)
1524 South IH 35, Suite 205
Austin, TX 78704
Phone: (512) 499-8248
Fax: (512) 499-8264
Website: http://www.txgifted.org

Texas Education Agency
1701 N. Congress Avenue
Austin, TX 78701
Phone: (512) 463-9734
Website: http://www.tea.state.tx.us/index.aspx

Division of Advanced Academic Services
Phone: (512) 463-9581
E-mail: curric@tea.state.tx.us
Website: http://www.tea.state.tx.us/gted

Utah

Utah Association for Gifted Children (UAGC)
Sheri Sorensen, President
P.O. Box 9332
Salt Lake City, UT 84109
Phone: (801) 635-5780
E-mail: sasorensen@graniteschools.org
Website: http://www.uagc.org

Utah State Office of Education
250 E. 500 South
P.O. Box 144200
Salt Lake City, UT 84114
Phone: (801) 538-7500
Website: http://www.usoe.k12.ut.us

Gifted and Talented
Moya Kessig
E-mail: moya.kessig@schools.utah.gov
Website: http://www.usoe.k12.ut.us/curr/gift_talent

Vermont

Vermont Council for Gifted Education
Ellen Koier, President
P.O. Box 154
Peacham, VT 05862
E-mail: vcgepres@vcge.org
Website: http://www.vcge.org

Vermont Department of Education
120 State Street
Montpelier, VT 05620
Phone: (802) 828-3135
E-mail: DOE-edinfo@state.vt.us
Website: http://www.education.vermont.gov

Virginia

Virginia Association for the Gifted
Liz Nelson, Executive Director
P.O. Box 26212
Richmond, VA 23260
Phone: (804) 355-5945
Fax: (804) 355-5137
E-mail: vagifted@comcast.net
Website: http://www.vagifted.org

Virginia Department of Education
P.O. Box 2120
Richmond, VA 23218
Phone: (800) 292-3820
Website: http://www.doe.virginia.gov

Gifted Education
Donna L. Poland
Office of Middle and High School Instruction
Phone: (804) 225-2884
Fax: (804) 786-5466
E-mail: Donna.Poland@doe.virginia.gov
Website: http://www.doe.virginia.gov/instruction/gifted_ed/index.
shtml

Washington

Washington Association of Educators of the Talented and Gifted (WAETAG)
Mary Freitas, President
830 Cary Road
Edmonds, WA 98020
E-mail: m-freitas@lycos.com
Website: http://www.waetag.net

Northwest Gifted Child Association
P.O. Box 10704
Spokane, WA 99209
Website: http://www.nwgca.org

Office of Superintendent of Public Instruction (OSPI)
Old Capitol Building
P.O. Box 47200
600 Washington Street SE
Olympia, WA 98504
Phone: (360) 725-6000
TTY: (360) 664-3631
Website: http://www.k12.wa.us

Gifted and Talented Education
Barbara Dittrich, Supervisor, Advanced Placement
Phone: (360) 725-6097
E-mail: barbara.dittrich@k12.wa.us
Website: http://www.k12.wa.us/AdvancedPlacement/default.aspx

West Virginia

West Virginia Association for the Gifted and Talented (WVAGT)
Patti Coon, President
E-mail: padc78@hotmail.com
Website: http://www.wvgifted.org

West Virginia Department of Education
1900 Kanawha Boulevard East
Charleston, WV 25305
Website: http://wvde.state.wv.us

Office of Special Programs, Extended and Early Learning
Phone: (304) 558-2696
E-mail: lboyer@access.k12.wv.us
Website: http://wvde.state.wv.us/osp

Wisconsin

Wisconsin Association for Talented and Gifted (WATG)
Nancy Woodward, Executive Assistant, WATG
1553 Smithfield Drive
Sun Prairie, WI 53590
Phone: (608) 318-0671
Fax: (608) 318-0725
E-mail: watg@watg.org
Website: http://www.watg.org

Wisconsin Department of Public Instruction
Tony Evers, State Superintendent of Public Instruction
125 S. Webster Street
P.O. Box 7841
Madison, WI 53707
Phone: (800) 441-4563
Website: http://dpi.wi.gov

Gifted and Talented
Chrystyna V. Mursky
Phone: (608) 267-9273
E-mail: Chrystyna.Mursky@dpi.wi.gov
Website: http://dpi.wi.gov/cal/gifted.html

Wyoming

Wyoming State Department of Education
Hathaway Building, 2nd Floor
2300 Capitol Avenue
Cheyenne, WY 82002
Phone: (307) 777-7690
Fax: (307) 777-6234
Website: http://www.k12.wy.us

Canadian National Organizations

Canadian Council for Exceptional Children
Website: http://www.cec.sped.org/Content/NavigationMenu/
AboutCEC/Communities/Canada

Canadian Centers for Gifted Education

Centre for Gifted Education
University of Calgary
Education Tower, 602
Calgary, AB, Canada, T2N 1N4
Phone: (403) 220-7799
Fax: (403) 210-2068
E-mail: gifted@ucalgary.ca
Website: http://gifted.ucalgary.ca/

Canadian Associations and Departments of Education

Alberta

Alberta Associations for Bright Children (AABC/Alberta)
Website: http://www.edmontonabc.org/aabc/

Alberta Education (Alberta Government)
Commerce Place, 7th Floor
10155 102 Street
Edmonton, AB, Canada T5J 4L5
Phone: (780) 427-7219
Website: http://education.alberta.ca

Special Programs Branch (Gifted and Talented)
Website: http://education.alberta.ca/admin/special/ecs.aspx

British Columbia

Gifted Children's Association of British Columbia
Melinda Meszaros, President
2772 East Broadway
Vancouver, BC V5M IY8
Phone or Fax: (877) 707-6111
Website: http://www.gcabc.ca

British Columbia Ministry of Education
P.O. Box 9149, Stn Prov Govt
Victoria, BC, Canada, V8W 9H8
Phone: (888) 879-1166
E-mail: enquirybc@gov.bc.ca
Website: http://www.gov.bc.ca/bced

Manitoba

Manitoba Education and Literacy
Phone: (866) 626-4862
Fax: (204) 945-4261
E-mail: mgi@gov.mb.ca
Website: http://www.edu.gov.mb.ca

New Brunswick

The Association for Bright Children, New Brunswick Chapter
Carol Ann White, Co-chair
169 Chamberlain Road
Quispamsis, NB, Canada, E2G 1B7
Phone: (506) 847-4180
Website: http://www.sjfn.nb.ca/community_hall/A/asso4180.html

New Brunswick Department of Education
Place 2000
P.O. Box 6000
Fredericton, NB, Canada, E3B 5H1
Phone: (506) 453-3678
Fax: (506) 453-3325
E-mail: edcommunication@gnb.ca
Website: http://www.gnb.ca/0000/index-e.asp

Newfoundland

Newfoundland and Labrador Association for Gifted Children (NLAGC)
David McKenzie
61 Flats Road
CBS, NL, Canada, A1W 3C5
Phone: (709) 834-4051
E-mail: step3332003@yahoo.ca
Website: http://www.cdli.ca/nlagc/nlagc.html

Newfoundland and Labrador Department of Education
P.O. Box 8700
St. John's, NL, Canada, A1B 4J6
Phone: (709) 729-5097
Fax: (709) 729-5896
E-mail: education@gov.nl.ca
Website: http://www.ed.gov.nl.ca/edu

Northwest Territories

Government of the Northwest Territories: Education, Culture, and Employment
P.O. Box 1320
Yellowknife, NT, Canada, X1A 2L9
Phone: (867) 669-2366
Fax: (867) 873-0169
Website: http://www.ece.gov.nt.ca

Northwest Territories Teachers' Association
P.O. Box 2340
5018 48th Street
Yellowknife, NT, Canada, X1A 2P7
Phone: (867) 873-7222
Fax: (867) 873- 0107
E-mail: nwtta@nwtta.nt.ca
Website: http://www.nwtta.nt.ca

Nova Scotia

Association for Bright Children of Nova Scotia
David W. Richey
P.O. Box 723
Dartmouth, NS, Canada, B2Y 3Z3
Phone: (902) 465-4481
Fax: (902) 463-4319
E-mail: rfurling@gcameronassoc.com
Nova Scotia Department of Education
P.O. Box 578
2021 Brunswick Street, Suite 402
Halifax, NS, Canada, B3J 2S9
Phone: (902) 424-5168
Fax: (902) 424-0511
Website: http://www.ednet.ns.ca

Ontario

Association for Bright Children of Ontario
P.O. Box 59088
2238 Dundas St West
Toronto, ON, Canada, M6R 3B5
E-mail: abcinfo@abcontario.ca
Website: http://www.abcontario.ca

Ontario Gifted
P.O. Box 2473
Richmond Hill, ON, Canada, L4E 1A5
Phone: (905) 313-1140
Website: http://www.sparkedonline.com

Ontario Ministry of Education
Public Inquiries Unit
880 Bay Street, 2nd Floor
Toronto, ON, Canada, M7A 1N3
Phone: (800) 387-5514
Fax: (416) 325-6348
E-mail: info@edu.gov.on.ca
Website: http://www.edu.gov.on.ca/eng

Prince Edward Island

Prince Edward Island Department of Education
Holman Centre
250 Water Street, Suite 101
Summerside, PE, Canada, C1N 1B6
Phone: (902) 438-4130
Fax: (902) 438-4062
E-mail: island@gov.pe.ca
Website: http://www.gov.pe.ca/eecd

Québec

Ministère de l'Éducation/Education Québec
1035 rue De La Chevrotière
Québec, QC, Canada, G1R 5A5
Phone: (418) 644-1259
Fax: (418) 646-9170
Website: http://www.meq.gouv.qc.ca/GR-PUB/m_englis.htm

Saskatchewan

Saskatchewan Education
2220 College Avenue
Regina, SK, Canada, S4P4V9
Phone: (306) 787-6030
Website: http://www.education.gov.sk.ca

Saskatchewan Teachers' Federation
2317 Arlington Avenue
Saskatoon, SK, Canada, S7J 2H8
Phone: (306) 373 1660
Fax: (306) 374-1122
E-mail: stf@stf.sk.ca
Website: http://www.stf.sk.ca

Yukon

Government of Yukon: Department of Education
P.O. Box 2703
Whitehorse, YK, Canada, Y1A 2C6
Phone: (867) 667-5141
Fax: (867) 393-6254
E-mail: contact.education@gov.yk.ca
Website: http://www.education.gov.yk.ca

ABOUT THE AUTHOR

Tracy L. Cross, Ph.D., holds an endowed chair as the Jody and Layton Smith Professor of Psychology and Gifted Education and is the executive director of the Center for Gifted Education at The College of William and Mary. Previously he served Ball State University as the George and Frances Ball Distinguished Professor of Psychology and Gifted Studies, the executive director of the Center for Gifted Studies and Talent Development, and at the Institute for Research on the Psychology of Gifted Students. For 9 years he served as the executive director of the Indiana Academy for Science, Mathematics, and Humanities, a residential high school for intellectually gifted adolescents. He has published more than 150 articles and book chapters and 40 columns, has made more than 200 presentations at conferences, and has published four books. He has edited five journals in the field of gifted studies and is the current editor of the *Journal for the Education of the Gifted*. He received the Distinguished Service Award from The Association for the Gifted and the National Association for Gifted Children (NAGC), the Early Leader and Early Scholar Awards from NAGC, and the Lifetime Achievement Award from the MENSA Education and Research Foundation.

ABOUT THE CONTRIBUTORS

 **Laurence J. Coleman, Ph.D.,** is the Daso Herb Professor of Gifted Education and a member of the Department of Early Childhood, Physical and Special Education at The University of Toledo. He is a special education teacher who became a teacher, educator, and researcher. He is past editor of the *Journal for the Education of the Gifted* (1994–2005) and teaches courses in theoretical analysis, gifted education, and qualitative inquiry. Among his many professional activities, he is proud of creating an innovative model of teaching as a talent; building the Summer Institute for Gifted Children in 1980, which has been "taken over" by the original students and is still in operation; receiving the Distinguished Scholar Award from the National Association for Gifted Children and the Outstanding Service Award from The Association for the Gifted of the Council for Exceptional Children; and publishing *Being Gifted in School* with Tracy Cross and *Nurturing Talent in High School: Life in the Fast Lane.* Dr. Coleman's scholarly interests are the experience of being gifted, program evaluation, and teacher thinking. He is principal investigator of a 5-year, longitudinal study funded by the U.S. Department of Education, "Accelerating Achievement in Math and Science in Urban Schools."

Sal Mendaglio, Ph.D., is a professor in the Faculty of Education, University of Calgary. For more than 20 years, he taught in the Department of Educational Psychology, contributing to the preparation of psychologists. Ten years ago, he began teaching in the Division of Teacher Preparation in which he held the position of Assistant Dean. Sal also teaches graduate courses in gifted education in the Graduate Division of Educational Research. He is cofounder of the Centre for Gifted Education, which has recently celebrated its 20th anniversary. He currently holds the position of research associate with the Centre. His passion is counseling gifted individuals, which he began more than 30 years ago. Models of counseling gifted youth and Dabrowski's theory of positive disintegration are topics of his recent publications.

Maureen Neihart, Psy.D., is a licensed clinical child psychologist with more than 25 years' experience counseling high-ability children and their families. She is coeditor of the text *The Social and Emotional Development of Gifted Children: What Do We Know?* and a former member of the board of directors of the National Association for Gifted Children. Dr. Neihart serves on the editorial boards of *Gifted Child Quarterly, Roeper Review,* and *The Journal of Secondary Gifted Education,* and has given more than 300 lectures and workshops worldwide. She is currently Associate Professor and Head of Psychological Studies at the National Institute of Education in Singapore, where her interests include the social and emotional development of gifted children, home- and school-based psychological interventions for children at risk, resilience, and the psychology of high performance. Her most recent books are *Peak Performance for Smart Kids* and *Gifted Children With Autism Spectrum Disorders*, both published by Prufrock Press. Dr. Neihart fantasizes about living a literary life. Her one-act comedy, *The Court Martial of George Armstrong Custer*, was produced and filmed for local U.S. television in 2000.

Paula Olszewski-Kubilius, Ph.D., is currently director of the Center for Talent Development at Northwestern University and a professor in the School of Education and Social Policy. Over the past 26 years, she has created programs for all kinds of gifted learners and written extensively on issues of talent development, particularly on programs to serve underrepresented gifted students. She has served as the editor of *Gifted Child Quarterly*, as coeditor of *The Journal of Secondary Gifted Education*, and on the editorial review boards of *Gifted and Talented International*, *Roeper Review*, and *Gifted Child Today*. She also serves on the board of trustees of the Illinois Mathematics and Science Academy and the Illinois Association for the Gifted. She is currently vice president and president-elect of the National Association for Gifted Children. She is the recipient of the Distinguished Scholar Award (2009) from the National Association for Gifted Children.

Nancy M. Robinson, Ph.D., is Professor Emerita of Psychiatry and Behavioral Sciences at the University of Washington and former director of what is now known as the Halbert and Nancy Robinson Center for Young Scholars, a center established in 1975 by her late husband. Known previously for a 30-year career in intellectual disabilities (formerly termed mental retardation), her research interests since 1981 have focused on effects of marked academic acceleration to college, adjustment issues of gifted children, intellectual assessment, and verbal and mathematical precocity in very young children. For many years, she worked with families and children at both ends of the intellectual spectrum. She has consulted for more than 20 years with independent schools around the world in conjunction with the U.S. State Department's Office of Overseas Schools. She received the 1998 NAGC Distinguished Scholar Award and the 2007 NAGC Ann Isaacs Founders Memorial Award.

Mary Ann Swiatek, Ph.D., has been doing research on giftedness since exploring the topic of acceleration in a library research project as an undergraduate in the late 1980s. She graduated from Oberlin College with honors in psychology and immediately went on to Iowa State University, from which she received her M.S. and Ph.D. in counseling psychology. While at Iowa State, she was fortunate to work with Dr. Camilla Benbow and the Study of Mathematically Precocious Youth (SMPY). Since receiving her doctorate, she has worked as a college professor at SUNY Fredonia and Lafayette College, and as a research specialist with the Carnegie Mellon Institute for Talented Elementary and Secondary Students (C-MITES). Currently, she is a psychologist at KidsPeace, a large psychiatric facility for children and adolescents. She is a past member of the board of the Pennsylvania Association for Gifted Education (PAGE) and continues to be an active member of the PAGE Speakers Bureau. Her interests focus on academic acceleration and social coping among gifted students, but she regularly speaks on other topics related to giftedness as well.

 **Rena F. Subotnik, Ph.D.,** is director of the Center for Gifted Education Policy at the American Psychological Association. The center's mission is to generate public awareness, advocacy, clinical applications, and cutting-edge research ideas that will enhance the achievement and performance of children and adolescents with special gifts and talents in all domains. She is coeditor of *Developing Giftedness and Talent Across the Life Span* (with F.D. Horowitz and D. Matthews), *Methodologies for Conducting Research on Giftedness* (with Bruce Thompson), *The International Handbook of Research on Giftedness and Talent* (2nd edition, with F. Mönks, K. Heller, and R. J. Sternberg), *Remarkable Women: Perspectives on Female Talent Development* (with K. Arnold and K. Noble), and *Beyond Terman: Contemporary Longitudinal Studies of Giftedness and Talent* (with K. Arnold). She also is the first author of *Genius Revisited: High IQ Children Grown Up* (with L. Kassan, A. Wasser, and E. Summers).